ELEMENTARY GRAMMAR
Worksheets

ANDY and AUDREY JACKSON

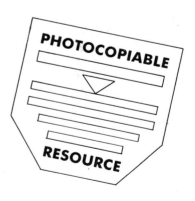

PHOTOCOPIABLE RESOURCE

Prentice Hall

New York   London   Toronto   Sydney   Tokyo   Singapore

PRENTICE HALL INTERNATIONAL ENGLISH LANGUAGE TEACHING

First published 1992 by
Prentice Hall International (UK) Ltd
Campus 400, Maylands Avenue
Hemel Hempstead
Hertfordshire, HP2 7EZ
A division of
Simon & Schuster International Group

Typeset in 10/12pt Century Schoolbook by Taurus Graphics,
Abingdon, Oxon

Printed and bound in Great Britain by Dotesios Ltd, Trowbridge,
Wiltshire.

Illustrations by Harry Venning

British Library Cataloguing in Publication Data
A catalogue record for this book is available from the British
Library

ISBN 0–13–253295–6

2 3 4 5 96 95 94 93

Contents

428.24JAC

PHO

▭ Worksheets marked with this symbol have accompanying cassette tape drills. The tapescripts for these drills are at the end of the book. They are numbered 1 to 22.

Introduction

These worksheets form the first level of a structural self-access system. They are intended for elementary students of English and deal with most of the basic grammatical points covered in elementary course books, giving a brief explanation or illustration of each point before providing a practice exercise, with the answers inverted at the bottom of the page. They present broad rules, leaving the exceptions and more complex explanations to grammar and course books. They are not intended as an alternative to a course book or a grammar, which are more comprehensive in their explanations and exercises, and of which there is now a wide choice on the market. The purpose is to offer students the opportunity to practise individual grammatical points on their own in a simple style, in order to consolidate an initial model of the language. They are designed to be photocopied and placed in self-access or resources centres, and to be written on by the students and corrected by themselves. For this reason, they are in A4 format, with simple line drawings for illustration and ample space for students to write in their answers. They could also be used by teachers to follow up lessons, rather than allowing students to write in the textbook, where the space provided for writing is often inadequate. In this case, the teachers may wish to cover up the answer section while photocopying, and go over the answers in class.

There is a simple glossary sheet (overleaf) giving illustrations of the terms used which students should use in association with the worksheets, and on sheet 68 there is a list of irregular verbs with a space for students to write in their translation of the verbs.

The accompanying cassette provides simple drills, revising much of the vocabulary used in the exercises, in order to give students the opportunity to listen to and pronounce new words or structures in association with the writing exercises. Not all the Worksheets have related cassette exercises but teachers are advised to make extra copies of Worksheets with cassette symbols to place in their listening centre.

Note that the Worksheets are arranged in alphabetical order for ease of reference and for filing in the resource centre.

Glossary

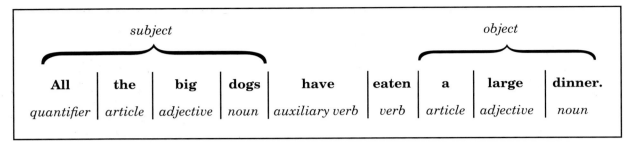

adjective	nice, tall, comfortable, green	The *fat* lady had a *new* dress.
adverb	easily, often, heavily, fast	The boys *never* play *quietly*.
article	the, a, this	*The* boy climbed *a* tree.
auxiliary verb	have, be, do, was, did	They *have* made a mistake.
conditional	if	It will break *if* you drop it.
conjunction	and, but, so, when, as soon as	He smiled *as* he walked out.
gerund	going, writing, playing	He likes *singing*.
infinitive	(to) go, (to) write	You must *stay* with us.
modal	can, must, should	It *may* rain tonight.
noun	man, idea, table, freedom	This *book* tells a good *story*.
passive	is done, was done	The window *was broken* last night.
phrasal verb	make for, look after	She *got over* her illness quickly.
preposition	at, in, under, before, of	I'll be *in* the house *at* six.
present tense	is doing, does	He *is working* hard as he always *does*.
present perfect	has done, has been doing	We *have been waiting* for a long time.
pronoun	I, we, them, myself, mine	*She* can do *it herself*.
quantifier	some, both, a few	*None* of them has *any* money.
tense	is, was, will be	It *will be* ready when they *come*.
verb	eat, swim, break	He *worked* very hard.

1 Adjectives: position

a *tall* man, a *big* house

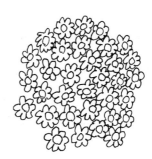

This is Mr Adams.
He is a policeman.
He is fat.
Mr Adams is a fat policeman.

This is Miss Brookes.
She is a nurse.
She is tall.
Miss Brookes is a tall nurse.

These are daisies.
They are small.
Daisies are small flowers.

Exercise A

Example: Mary / girl / young   *Mary is a young girl.*

1 David / man / old

2 New York / city / big

3 Elephants / animals / large

4 Peas / vegetables / green

5 Marlon Brando / actor / famous

Exercise B

Nouns: weights building car birds swimmer sheep men

Adjectives: white old heavy tall black fast strong

Use these nouns and adjectives in the following sentences:

Examples:

 This is a white   sheep.
                     (adjective) (noun)

 These are heavy   weights.
                     (adjective) (noun)

 1 These are _____ .

 2 This is a _____ .

 3 This is a _____ .

 4 This is a _____ .

 5 These are _____ .

Spelling rules for comparatives

- For one syllable words with one vowel and one consonant at the end, double the last consonant and add *er*
  big – bigger   fat – fatter   hot – hotter   sad – sadder   thin – thinner
- For one syllable words with one or two vowels or ending in two consonants, just add *er*
  long – longer   tall – taller   black – blacker   weak – weaker   soon – sooner
- For words of one or two syllables ending with *e*, just add *r*.
  nice – nicer   wide – wider   simple – simpler
- For words of two syllables ending with a consonant and *y*, change the *y* to *i* and add *er*.
  pretty – prettier   easy – easier   funny – funnier   smelly – smellier
- For most three syllable words and all longer ones, use *more*.
  capable – more capable   intelligent – more intelligent   difficult – more difficult

| Mr Adams | Miss Brookes | Mr Church | Ms Dangerfield |
| A | B | C | D |

Examples: Mr Adams is *older than* Miss Brookes.
Miss Brookes is *prettier than* Ms Dangerfield.
Ms Dangerfield is *more intelligent than* Miss Brookes.
Mr Church is *more handsome than* Mr Adams.

Exercise A

Make sentences about the people above:

Example: fat   A / C   Mr Adams is fatter than Mr Church.

   1   thin   B / D   _____
   2   happy   C / A   _____
   3   sad   D / B   _____
   4   rich   C / A   _____
   5   poor   D / B   _____
   6   intelligent   A / B   _____
   7   strong   C / D   _____

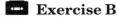 ### Exercise B

Do Exercise 1 on the cassette.

3 Adjectives: possessive

my family, *her* book

I – my book	he – his book	we – our book	Mary – Mary's book
you – your book	she – her book	they – their book	Jack – Jack's book

The Smith's family tree

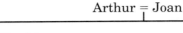

Arthur = Joan

Mary = David   Louise = Fred

Sue   Peter   Joe   Anne

Fred   Mary   Louise   Arthur   Joan
Anne   Sue   David   Peter   Joe

Exercise A

Diane is talking to Mary. Use the family tree above to fill in the gaps.

Example:
Diane: Who is the man in the centre?   Mary: It's _____*my*_____ husband, David.

1   Is Joan your sister?   No, she's _____ mother!

2   And is Anne your daughter?   No, she's _____ niece.

3   Is Peter her brother?   No, he's _____cousin.

4   And who's Joe?   He's _____ brother.

5   Is Louise Fred's sister?   No, she's _____ wife.

6   So is Louise _____ sister?   Yes, she is.

7   And Peter is _____son?   Yes, he is.

8   So that means David is Peter
    and Sue's uncle?   No, he's _____ husband, _____father!

9   And this person, Arthur, is your and
    Louise's brother?   No, he's _____ father.

    Your mother looks very young!
    You have a nice family.   Thank you.

Exercise B

Do Exercise 2 on the cassette.

4 Adjectives: superlative

the *biggest*

Spelling rules for superlatives

- For one syllable words with one vowel and one consonant at the end, double the last consonant and add *est*.

  big – biggest   fat – fattest   hot – hottest   sad – saddest   thin – thinnest

- For one syllable words ending in two consonants or with two vowels, just add *est*.

  long – longest   tall – tallest   black – blackest   weak – weakest

- For words of one or two syllables ending with *e*, just add *st*.

  nice – nicest   wide – widest   simple – simplest

- For words of two syllables ending with a consonant and *y*, change the *y* to *i* and add *est*.

  pretty – prettiest   easy – easiest   funny – funniest   smelly – smelliest

- For most three syllable words and all longer ones, use *most*.

  capable – most capable   intelligent – most intelligent   difficult – most difficult

---

Exercise A

Arthur, Brenda, Charles and Delia are friends.

Examples: Arthur is *the tallest* of the four. Brenda is *the happiest* of the four. Charles is the oldest of the four. Delia is the *most intelligent* of the four.

Make sentences like the examples.

1   Charles – fat   _____

2   Delia – slim   _____

3   Arthur – strong   _____

4   Brenda – elegant   _____

Exercise B

Example: High mountains (world): Mont Blanc / Everest / Kilimanjaro
Everest is the highest mountain *in* the world.

Make sentences like the example.

1   Long rivers (Europe): the Danube / the Rhine / the Seine

_____

2   Big animals (Africa): the rhino / the elephant / the hippopotamus

_____

3   Busy airports (England): Gatwick / Heathrow / Manchester

_____

4   Expensive metals (world): platinum / silver / gold

_____

5   Fast passenger planes (world): Concorde / the 747 / the Airbus

_____

Exercise C

Do Exercise 3 on the cassette.

ANSWERS

A 1 Charles is the fattest of the four. **2** Delia is the slimmest of the four. **3** Arthur is the strongest of the four. **4** Brenda is the most elegant of the four.
B 1 The Danube is the longest river in Europe. **2** The elephant is the biggest animal in Africa. **3** Heathrow is the busiest airport in England. **4** Platinum is the most expensive metal in the world. **5** Concorde is the fastest passenger plane in the world.

5 Adjectives: plus prepositions

I'm *interested in* . . .

Some adjectives in English are often followed by a special preposition.

PLEASED WITH: My mother was very *pleased with* me because I passed my exams. (person)

PLEASED ABOUT: My father was very *pleased about* his new job. (thing)

WORRIED ABOUT: The doctor is *worried about* my brother. He's very ill.

GOOD/BAD AT;   Yoko is very *good at* sport but *bad at* languages.

READY FOR: My suitcase is packed and I'm *ready for* a holiday.

DIFFERENT FROM: American English is not very *different from* British English, but they say 'different than' in America!

INTERESTED IN: Peter is very *interested in* football; he plays twice a week.

AFRAID OF: Many people are *afraid of* spiders, but most of them are not dangerous.

TIRED OF: We're *tired of* this game. Let's do something else.

USED TO: Don't stay too long in the sun until you are *used to* it.

Exercise A

Choose the best adjective and preposition from the list above for each sentence.

1   You don't need to be _____ _____ the dog: it doesn't bite.

2   The farmers are _____ _____ their crops because it hasn't rained for weeks.

3   My sister was _____ _____ the present I got her. She loves it.

4   If you are not _____ _____ exercise, you should go carefully at first.

5   Your new car is very _____ _____ your last one. It's much better!

6   I'm really _____ _____ tennis: I lose every game I play.

7   I'll just put my shoes on and then I'll be _____ _____ a walk.

8   Our boss was _____ _____ our hard work, and gave us a holiday.

9   She is so _____ _____ mathematics, she gets 100% in all her exams.

10   If you are not _____ _____ this kind of drama, why did you come to the theatre?

If you want to use a verb after the adjective and preposition, it must end in (*ing*).
Example: I am very interested in work(ing) abroad.
Greta is very good at play(ing) the violin.
My French friend is not used to driv(ing) on the left in England.

Exercise B

Write in the correct preposition and then choose the best verb from the list below to complete these sentences.

1   My little brother is afraid _____ _____ on his own so we share a bedroom.

2   Jeanne is worried _____ _____ her exams, so she is working very hard.

3   Playing professional football is very different _____ _____ in an amateur league.

4   Ben is bad _____ _____ lies. He always goes red in the face.

5   I'm tired _____ _____ the dinner. Why don't you do it today?

failing / cooking / telling / sleeping / playing

ANSWERS
A 1 afraid of; 2 worried about; 3 pleased about; 4 used to; 5 different from; 6 bad at; 7 ready for; 8 pleased with; 9 good at; 10 interested in
B 1 of sleeping; 2 about failing; 3 from playing; 4 at telling; 5 of cooking

6 Adverbs: formation

She plays *beautifully*.

ADJECTIVE				ADVERB
strong		+ *ly* =		strongly
cheerful		+ *ly* =		cheerfully
happy	y > i	+ *ly* =		happily

Example: Susan is a careful driver. *She drives carefully.*

Exercise A

Make a sentence for each picture.

1   John is a quick runner.   He _____

2   Mohammed is a brave fighter.   He _____

3   Geoffrey is a bad writer.   He _____

4   Maria is a beautiful singer.   She _____

5   Sheila is a strong swimmer.   She _____

6   Andy is a noisy eater.   He _____

7   Ilanova is a graceful dancer.   She _____

8   Ann is a dangerous driver.   She _____

9   Joe is a careless painter.   He _____

10 The bird is a loud singer.   It _____

Exercise B

Do Exercise 4 on the cassette.

ANSWERS
A 1 He runs quickly. 2 He fights bravely. 3 He writes badly. 4 She sings beautifully. 5 She swims strongly. 6 He eats noisily. 7 She dances gracefully. 8 She drives dangerously. 9 He paints carelessly. 10 It sings loudly.

7 Adverbs: position

She *never* goes to the cinema.

ADVERBS tell us more about the VERB in a sentence. We usually put them *after the OBJECT*, if there is one.

Examples:

Carmen plays
the violin *beautifully*.

Julio placed the box
carefully on the floor.

The cows walked *slowly*
along the road.

However, some adverbs, which tell us *how often*, come *between the SUBJECT and the VERB*. Here are some of the common ones:

always / usually / frequently / often / sometimes / occasionally / rarely / never

Examples: Banks *never* open on Sundays.
The boss *occasionally* comes to work late.

Rewrite the following in the correct order to make good sentences.

Example: quickly / the door / Simon / opened

Simon opened the door quickly.

1 all day / the soldiers / bravely / fought

2 mistakes / our teacher / rarely / makes

3 on time / never / arrives / this train

4 on the floor / Ben / his clothes / carelessly / dropped

5 his gun / in the air / dangerously / waved / the soldier

6 brushes / Anna / her teeth / always / before bed

7 held / the little girl / tightly / her mother's hand

8 the injured man / gently / examined / the doctor

9 neatly / her car / between two lorries / parked / Birgit

10 play / tennis / the boys / on Wednesdays / usually

11 late / works / Catherine / often

12 yesterday / was shining / the sun / brightly

8 Articles: indefinite

What is this? – It is *a/an . . .*

	consonants		*vowels*
	b c d f g h j k l m n p q r s t v w x y z		**a e i o u**
a man			an apple
a car			an egg
			an island
a woman			an orange
			an umbrella

Exercise A

Write *a* or *an*.
Example: *a* bed   *an* office

1 _____ house   2 _____ fish   3 _____ ice-cream   4 _____ mountain   5 _____ igloo

6 _____ taxi   7 _____ ashtray   8 _____ book   9 _____ elephant   10 _____ pen

Exercise B

What is this / that?
Write the question and answer.

It is   *a / an* _____ .

1 What is this?   ___ ___ ___ ___

2 What is that?   ___ ___ ___ ___

3 _____ _____ _____ ?   ___ ___ ___ ___

4 _____ _____ _____ ?   ___ ___ ___ ___

5 _____ _____ _____ ?   ___ ___ ___ ___

6 _____ _____ _____ ?   ___ ___ ___ ___

7 _____ _____ _____ ?   ___ ___ ___ ___

8 _____ _____ _____ ?   ___ ___ ___ ___

9 _____ _____ _____ ?   ___ ___ ___ ___

10 _____ _____ _____ ?   ___ ___ ___ ___

ANSWERS
A 1 a; 2 a; 3 an; 4 a; 5 an; 6 a; 7 an; 8 a; 9 an; 10 a.
B 1 It is a book. 2 It is an elephant. 3 What is this? It is an umbrella. 4 What is this? It is an ashtray. 5 What is that? It is a fish. 6 What is that? It is an igloo. 7 What is this? It is an ice-cream. 8 What is that? It is a house. 9 What is this? It is a taxi. 10 What is that? It is a mountain.

9 Articles: definite

The Grand Hotel in London

> We use *the* when we know which person or thing we are talking about. (*the girl over there*)
>
> We use *the* when there is only one example. (*the President of France, the Pope*)
>
> We use *the* with the names of hotels, museums, public buildings or rivers.
>
> (*the Hilton Hotel / the British Museum / the Central Library / the Mississipi*)
>
> BUT
>
> We do not use *the* with *the* names of streets, stations, towns, mountains or countries.
> (*Oxford Street / Victoria Station / Berlin / Everest / Turkey*)
>
> *Exceptions*: We say *the UK*, *the USA* and *the West Indies*.

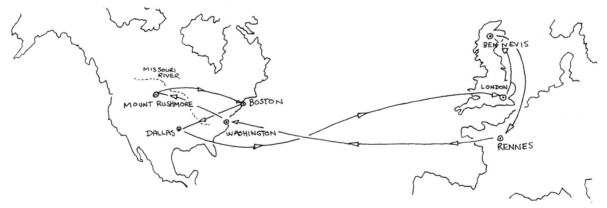

Put *the* in the gaps in the text **only where necessary**.

Michel lives in (1) _____ Rennes, a town in the west of (2) _____ France. He has a flat on the bank of (3) _____ Rance, a river which flows through (4) _____ centre of (5) _____ town. He is a journalist, and last year he visited (6) _____ Washington, (7) _____ capital of (8) _____ United States. He spent a lot of time in (9) _____ Smithsonian Museum doing research. He saw (10) _____ President outside (11) _____ White House, but didn't meet him. Then he travelled around (12) _____ States for three weeks, visiting places such as (13) _____ Mount Rushmore, (14) _____ Boston and (15) _____ Dallas, and he took a boat trip on (16) _____ Missouri.

On the way home, he spent five days in (17) _____ UK, including two days in (18) _____ London. He did a lot of shopping in (19) _____ Oxford Street, and stayed in (20) _____ Grand Hotel. He even had time to visit (21) _____ Scotland, but was not able to climb (22) _____ Ben Nevis, because (23) _____ weather was too bad. When he got home he was very tired!

10 Articles: demonstrative

this and *that, these* and *those*

this bottle	that bottle	these bottles	those bottles

Exercise A

Mr and Mrs Smith are returning from holiday.   They are going through customs at the airport.

Examples: What's *this*?   *It's a* camera.

What are *these*?   *They're* cigarettes.

1 _____ ?	_____ bottle of whisky.	
2 _____ ?	_____ chocolates.	
3 _____ ?	_____ presents.	
4 _____ ?	_____ watch.	
5 _____ ?	_____ box of cigars.	

Exercise B

Mr and Mrs Tanaka are on holiday in London.   They are talking to a tourist guide.

Examples: What's *that*?   *It's a* double-decker bus.

What are *those*?   *They're* pigeons.

1 _____ ?	_____ taxi.	
2 _____ ?	_____ traffic lights.	
3 _____ ?	_____ police officers.	
4 _____ ?	_____ post-box.	
5 _____ ?	_____ bus-stop.	

ANSWERS
A 1 What's this? It's a bottle of whisky. **2** What are these?
They're chocolates. **3** What are these? They're presents.
4 What's this? It's a watch. **5** What's this? It's a box of
cigars.

B 1 What's that? It's a taxi. **2** What are those? They're
traffic lights. **3** What are those? They're police officers.
4 What's that? It's a post-box. **5** What's that? It's a bus-
stop.

11 Conjunctions

John *and* Mary

<table>
<tr><td align="center">AND</td><td align="center">BUT</td></tr>
<tr><td align="center">+   +
–   –</td><td align="center">+   –
+   –</td></tr>
<tr><td>John is tall and Mary is tall.
I like ice-cream and you like chocolate.
Saudi Arabia is hot and sunny.
I am sad and you are lonely.</td><td>Tom is tall but Carol is short.
I like ice-cream but I don't like fish.
Sweden is small but strong.
She is rich but he is poor.</td></tr>
</table>

<table>
<tr><td align="center">SO (result)</td><td align="center">BECAUSE (reason)</td></tr>
<tr><td align="center">● → ●</td><td align="center">● ← ●</td></tr>
<tr><td>I'm tired so I'm going to bed.
It was wet so she stayed at home.
I like ice-cream so I eat a lot of it.</td><td>I'm going to bed because I'm tired.
She stayed at home because it was wet.
I eat ice-cream because I like it.</td></tr>
</table>

Join the pairs of sentences. Write *a* to *l* in the numbered spaces below.

1	The shop was closed	**a**	so we had a long swim.
2	My father shouted at me	**b**	but she hates sport.
3	The water was very warm	**c**	and it has green eyes.
4	Our cat has a long tail	**d**	and has a big car.
5	Mikki loves pop music	**e**	but I haven't finished.
6	The Nile is a very long river	**f**	because he was very angry.
7	They missed the bus	**g**	so we couldn't buy any cigarettes.
8	My boss was very pleased	**h**	because he is a good Muslim.
9	Tomoko asked me to a party	**i**	and it flows through many countries.
10	Mustapha prays five times a day	**j**	but I didn't want to go.
11	I've been working very hard	**k**	so they had to walk.
12	He lives in a large house	**l**	because I worked hard.

1 ____   2 ____   3 ____   4 ____   5 ____   6 ____

7 ____   8 ____   9 ____   10 ____   11 ____   12 ____

ANSWERS 1 g; 2 f; 3 a; 4 c; 5 b; 6 i; 7 k; 8 l; 9 j; 10 h; 11 e; 12 d.

12 Nouns: countable/uncountable

a *chair*, some *furniture*

All nouns in English are either countable or uncountable.
We can count tables and chairs, but we cannot count furniture.
We can count newspapers and books but we cannot count information.

COUNTABLE		UNCOUNTABLE
one table (is)	two tables (are)	(some) furniture (is)
a book (is)	three books (are)	(some) information (is)
an orange (is)	(some) oranges (are)	(some) fruit (is)

Here are some common examples:

COUNTABLE			UNCOUNTABLE		
vegetables	games	bottles	fruit	golf	liquid
apples	chairs	plates	ink	cheese	sugar
coins	pens	matches	money	furniture	tennis
cans	pencils	tables	oil	paper	
cups	notes		food	cash	

Exercise A

Jim is not married and he lives alone. He has no friends, so he only buys one of everything. Here is a picture of Jim's flat. Make a list of the numbered things in his flat. For countable things, write *a* or *an*. For uncountable things, write *some*.

1 _____ 6 _____

2 _____ 7 _____

3 _____ 8 _____

4 _____ 9 _____

5 _____ 10 _____

Exercise B

Do Exercise 5 on the cassette.

Exercise C

> If we want to count 'uncountable' nouns, we have to use an expression like *a bottle of* . . . or *a kilo of* . . . .

Draw a line to link the following uncountable nouns with the correct expression.

a bar of	a jar of	a bottle of	a loaf of	a bag of	a packet of	a litre of

bread	sugar	petrol	chocolate	coffee	milk	rice

13 Prepositions: direction

to the house, *along* the road, *down* the stairs

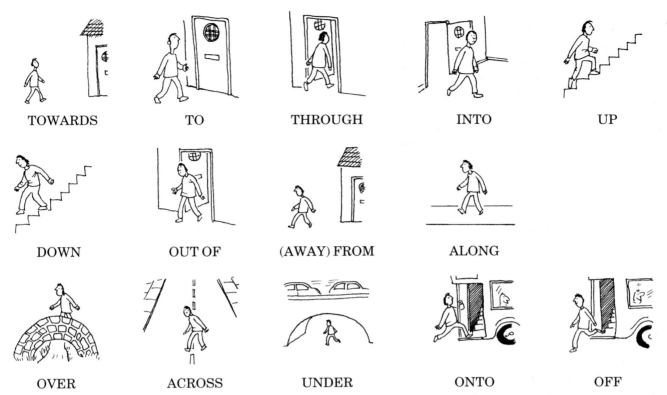

TOWARDS	TO	THROUGH	INTO	UP
DOWN	OUT OF	(AWAY) FROM	ALONG	
OVER	ACROSS	UNDER	ONTO	OFF

Exercise A

Pierre is a soldier. He must be very fit. Every day he has to train on an assault course.
Fill in the correct prepositions.

1 At 6.30 am Pierre goes _____ the start line.

2 Then he runs _____ a track _____ a river.

3 When he reaches the river, he climbs _____ a tree.

4 He goes _____ the river on a rope bridge.

5 Then he climbs _____ a wall and _____ a tunnel.

6 He goes _____ the tunnel.

7 When he comes _____ _____ it, he has to crawl

_____ barbed wire.

8 Then he runs _____ a hill and jumps

_____ a platform.

9 He has to jump _____ the platform

_____ the water.

10 Finally, he runs _____ the water and back

_____ the start line.

He is exhausted!

Exercise B

Do Exercise 6 on the cassette.

14 Prepositions: general

for me, *with* you, *by* us

WITH:	I went to the cinema *with* a friend. She opened the box *with* a knife.
WITHOUT:	Kurt prefers coffee *without* sugar. I can't do this *without* help.
BY:	Julia doesn't like travelling *by* train. I can do this *by* myself.
FOR:	they've been living here *for* three years. Is that present *for* Inga?

OF:	We ate half *of* the food. That dress is made *of* silk.
AT:	She's been *at* the dentist's today. The car was travelling *at* 80 kilometres an hour.
BECAUSE OF:	The match was stopped *because of* the bad weather. We were late *because of* the accident.
IN SPITE OF:	She enjoyed the walk *in spite of* the bad weather. *In spite of* my father's anger, I am going to go to the party.

Suzi is only fifteen but last week she decided to go to London.

Write in the correct prepositions.

1 Her mother wanted her to go _____ a friend.

2 But she went _____ herself.

3 She went _____ bus, because it was cheaper. She spent the morning shopping.

4 She bought a jacket made _____ soft green leather.

5 It was expensive, and _____ _____ the cost, she had very little money left.

6 It was a very hot afternoon, but _____ _____ _____ the high temperature, she wore her new jacket.

7 She walked around the streets _____ three hours.

8 When it was dark, she waited _____ the bus station, but there was no bus before 8 o'clock.

9 She finally got home _____ 11 o'clock. Her father was very angry.

15 Prepositions: place

at home *in* bed

AT	IN	ON
at home/work/school	*in* Rome (*town or city*)	*on* the table/shelf
at the beginning/end	*in* France (*country*)	*on* the ground/floor
at the theatre/cinema	*in* a car	*on* a bus/train/plane
at the station/airport	*in* a room/house/garden	*on* the wall/ceiling
at a party/dance/concert	*in* your tea/drink	*on* the left/right
	in bed/hospital/prison	
	in the air	

Exercise A

Write in the correct prepositions.

1 Where's John? He's not _____ work today.   No, he's _____ bed _____ hospital.

2 Where's your cup?   It's _____ the table.

3 Do you take sugar _____ your coffee?   No thanks.

4 Has the plane arrived _____ the airport?   No, it's still _____ the air.

5 Where were you last night, _____ a party?   No, I was _____ the theatre _____ London.

6 Have you seen my football?   Yes, it's _____ the grass _____ the garden.

7 Where do you live?   _____ Trento, a small town _____ Italy.

8 I can't find my shoes.   They're _____ the floor _____ the kitchen.

9 Did you meet him _____ the station?   No, he wasn't _____ the train.

10 Where is Mr Smith?   He's _____ the third room _____ the left.

Exercise B

Now look at the picture and answer the questions.
Example: Where is the car?   It's ___*in front of*___ the taxi.

1 Where is the taxi?   _____ the car and the bus.

2 Where is the plane?   _____ the helicopter.

3 Where is the bus?   _____ the taxi.

4 Where is the lorry?   _____ the bus.

5 Where is the helicopter?   _____ the plane.

6 Where is the boat?   _____ the lorry.

7 Where is the bicycle?   _____ the car.

8 Where is the dog?   _____ the car.

16 Prepositions: time

at four o'clock *on* Saturday

AT (*times / festivals*)	**ON** (*days / dates*)	**IN** (*months / years / seasons*)
at four o'clock *at* 3.15 *at* Christmas *at* the weekend	*on* Monday *on* 15th May *on* April 3rd	*in* July *in* 1992 *in* winter *in* the morning

Exercise A

Example: When does the plane leave?   *It leaves at 6.30.* _____

1   When did you arrive? _____

2   What time shall we start? _____

3   When do the shops close? _____

4   What time does the film begin? _____

Exercise B

Example: When is Christmas Day?   Friday   *Christmas Day is on 25th December.*

1   When is New Year's Day?   4th July   _____

2   When is American Independence Day?   25th December   _____

3   On which day do Christians go to church?   1st January   _____

4   On which day to Muslims go to the mosque? Sunday   _____

Exercise C

Fill in the gaps in the sentences with *on*, *in* or *at*.

1   _____ Monday, Susan woke up _____ five o'clock _____ the morning.

2   In England they play football _____ winter and cricket _____ summer.

3   My sister arrived _____ half past three _____ the afternoon.

4   I usually play badminton _____ Wednesdays and tennis _____ Saturdays.

Exercise D

Do Exercise 7 on the cassette.

17 Pronouns: compound

Is there *anybody* there?

There's somebody / someone in the house.

SOME · · ·

Positive verb

Is there anybody / anyone in the house?
There isn't anybody / anyone in the house.

ANY · · ·

Question or negative verb

There's nobody / no-one in the house.

NO · · ·

Positive verb

There's something in the box.

Is there anything in the box?
There isn't anything in the box.

There's nothing in the box.

Exercise A

Complete the following with:

somebody/someone   anybody/anyone   nobody/no-one   something/anything/nothing

1 Look! _____ has jumped into the river!

2 I didn't buy _____ in that shop.

3 Ouch! _____ in the sand has bitten me.

4 I'm really hungry but there's _____ in the fridge.

5 Did _____ see that film on TV last night?

6 She was very sad because _____ had remembered her birthday.

7 He didn't dance with _____ at the party.

8 I did my homework myself. _____ helped me.

9 I'm bored. I've got _____ to do.

10 What are we going to eat? I'll have to buy _____ for dinner.

Exercise B

Do Exercise 8 on the cassette.

18 Pronouns: personal

you and *I*

Hello. I am English. Are you English?

No. I am French.

subject	object
I	me
you	you
he	him
she	her
it	it
we	us
they	them

Fill in the gaps.

1 *A*: Hello, who are _____ ?

   B: _____ am a new student.

2 *A*: Welcome to the class. _____ am David and this is Maria. _____ is from Italy.

3 *B*: And who is that?

   A: That is Hans. _____ is from Germany.

4 *B*: And who are _____ ?

   A: _____ are new students from Qatar.

5 *C and D*: Hello. Are _____ a new student?

   B: Yes, _____ am.

   C and D: So are _____ . _____ are from Qatar.

6 *A*: Where is Qatar?

   D: _____ is near Saudi Arabia.

7 *D*: Do you know Maria?

   B: No, I don't know _____ .

8 *D*: Do you know the teacher?

   B: No, I don't know _____ .

9 *C and D*: Well, don't worry. Now you know _____ .

   B: Yes, and you know _____ , and soon I will know _____ as well.

19 Pronouns: possessive

my/mine

adjective	pronoun
my	mine
your	yours
his	his
her	hers
our	ours
their	theirs

Exercise A

The Smiths, Mary and David, are going on holiday with their children, Sue and Peter. They have four new suitcases, a red one, a blue one and two brown ones for the children. They must take them from the bus. Fill in the gaps.

David: Now, this is my suitcase, isn't it?

1 *Mary*: No, it's not _____, it's _____. I have the red

one. _____ is blue.

2 *David*: Yours? Well, where is _____?

3 *Peter*: Here's _____, Daddy, this blue one here.

4 *Sue*: No, that's not _____. It's this one.

5 *David*: Ah, good. Yes, this one is _____. Now, where are

_____, children?

6 *Mary*: _____ are brown, David. I think they are over there.

7 *David*: I see . . . These ones?

8 *Sue*: No, Daddy. Those are not _____. They're too big. These

ones here are _____.

9 *David*: Good. Now we have all _____. One, two, three,. . .

Where's Mummy's?

10 *Sue*: You are holding _____, Daddy.
    David: Oh yes, how silly of me!

Exercise B

Do Exercise 9 on the cassette.

20 Pronouns: reflexive

The little girl dressed *herself*.

I – myself	he – himself	she – herself	it – itself
you – yourself (*singular*)		you – yourselves (*plural*)	
we – ourselves		they – themselves	

Examples:

At first, the mother feeds the baby. Then, when the baby is older, *it can feed itself.*

David often takes a taxi, but sometimes *he drives himself.*

Exercise A

Finish the sentences, using each of these verbs once, with the correct reflexive pronoun.

hurt / dress / kill / clean / keep . . . warm / teach / cut / look after

1

Bill lit the fire to _____ .

2

Patricia is three. She can _____ now.

3

We are trying to _____ Chinese.

4

Don't play with that knife, Ron. You will _____ if you're not careful.

5

If you boys fall, you will _____ .

6

Don't worry, the children are old enough to _____ .

7

If he rides that motorbike as fast as that, he will surely _____ .

8

The cat _____ after every meal.

Exercise B

Do Exercise 10 on the cassette.

21 Quantifiers: a little/a few

I've got *a little* money.

COUNTABLE	UNCOUNTABLE
a few bottles	*a little* money
a few people	*a little* sugar
a few sweets	*a little* milk
There are *a few* biscuits on the plate.	There is *a little* water in the glass.

Exercise A

Complete the sentences with *a few* or *a little*.

1 There are only _____ students in the class. Where are the others?

2 There is _____ bread in the cupboard, but most of it has gone.

3 Can I have _____ sugar in my coffee? I don't like it without.

4 We ate _____ sandwiches and gave the rest to the birds.

5 There was _____ snow on the ground this morning. Winter is coming.

6 He only smoked _____ cigarettes today. He's slowly giving up.

7 I gave the cat _____ milk. It looked thirsty.

8 There were _____ people on the beach, although it was very early.

9 I only have _____ money in the bank, so I'm not having a holiday.

10 She's got _____ friends, so she is not usually lonely.

Exercise B

Do Exercise 11 on the cassette.

Andy and Audrey Jackson: Elementary Grammar Worksheets Photocopy Masters © Prentice Hall International (UK) Ltd 1992. All rights reserved

Both Tom and Jerry like ice-cream.
Neither Tom nor Jerry like(s) fish.
All the children like ice-cream.
None of the children like(s) fish.

	POSITIVE STATEMENTS	**NEGATIVE STATEMENTS**
Two people	**Both** . . . (and . . .) (+ plural verb)	Neither . . . (nor . . .) (+ plural or singular verb)
More than two people	All (+ plural verb)	None (+ plural or singular verb)

Examples:
Tom and Jerry are friends.
Both (of them) *like* ice cream. (They like ice-cream.)
Neither of them *like(s)* fish. (They don't like fish.)

Mr and Mrs Finn have five children.
All of them *like* ice-cream. (They like ice-cream.)
None of them *like(s)* fish. (They don't like fish.)

Complete the dialogue with *both*, *neither*, *all* or *none*.

Serge: Which of these shirts do you like? The red one or the yellow one?

Catherine: (1) _____ of them. I don't like the colours.

Serge: Well, I like (2) _____ of them. (3) _____ are made of cotton, and I prefer cotton.

Catherine: What about this white one, and this grey one?

  (4) _____ of these colours are smart.

Serge: But I don't want another smart shirt. (5) _____ of my shirts are smart. (6) _____ of them is casual. I need a casual shirt for the weekends.

Catherine: Well, (7) _____ of these shirts are expensive, so why don't you get (8) _____ of them? Then we'll (9) _____ be satisfied.

Serge: OK. I'll buy (10) _____ four of them.

Catherine: And when you wear the yellow one, I'll wear my sunglasses!

ANSWERS
1 Neither; 2 both; 3 Both; 4 Both; 5 All; 6 none; 7 none; 8 all; 9 both; 10 all

23 Quantifiers: a lot of/much/many

a lot of time, not *much* time, not *many* minutes

STATEMENT	NEGATIVE
a) Countables: I've got *a lot of* friends.	a) Countables: I haven't *many* friends.
b) Uncountables: I've got *a lot of* money.	b) Uncountables: I haven't got *much* money.

Syd

Arthur

John

Fred

Michael

Bill

David

Exercise A

Jane has a problem. She wants to get married, but doesn't know which man to choose.
Fill the gaps with *a lot of*, *much* or *many*.

John's got (1) _____ cars, but he hasn't got

(2) _____ patience.

David's got (3) _____ money, but he hasn't got (4) _____ friends.

Michael hasn't got (5) _____ money, but he's got

(6) _____ charm.

Arthur's (7) _____ fun, but he hasn't got (8) _____ sense
of fashion.

Bill hasn't got (9) _____ clothes, but he's (10) _____ fun.

Syd's got (11) _____ style, but he hasn't got

(12) _____ humour.

Fred hasn't got (13) _____ style, but he's got (14) _____ luck.

Jane is very lucky, because all the men love her and want to marry her

because she's got (15) _____ charm,

(16) _____ personality and (17) _____ nice friends. But

she hasn't got (18) _____ money, so she hasn't got

(19) _____ clothes, although she dresses with

(20) _____ elegance.

Which man do you think would be the best for her?

Exercise B

Do Exercise 12 on the cassette.

24

Quantifiers: so/such

It's not *so* difficult.

The car was *so expensive* that Tony couldn't buy it. It was *such an expensive car* that Tony couldn't buy it.

He ran *so quickly* that he won the race.

There were *so many* holes in his shirt that he threw it away.

SO	is followed by an *adjective* (so expensive) or an *adverb* (so quickly) or *much / many*
SUCH	is followed by *a(n) + adjective + noun* (an expensive car)

Complete the letter, putting in *so* or *such*.

```
                                                            c/Colom
                                                            Barcelona

                                                            19th March

Dear Kay,

   How are you? We're having a wonderful time here in Barcelona. It's

(1) _____ a beautiful city and the people are (2) _____ friendly.

The weather has been (3) _____ hot that we're already quite brown. The

streets are very crowded, though. There are (4) _____ many people that

it's difficult to cross the road, and the Spaniards drive (5) _____

quickly that I'm afraid we'll see an accident.

   I love Spain, though. It's (6) _____ an interesting country, with

(7) _____ much to see. Our guide is (8) _____ handsome and has

(9) _____ a good sense of humour that I never stop laughing. He says my

Spanish is (10) _____ bad that he is going to give me private lessons

. . . In fact, I'm thinking of staying in Spain and getting a job here!

Adios!

Love
Claire
```

Andy and Audrey Jackson: *Elementary Grammar Worksheets Photocopy Masters* © Prentice Hall International (UK) Ltd 1992. All rights reserved

25 Quantifiers: some/any

I've got *some*. Have you got *any*?

STATEMENT	NEGATIVE	QUESTION
a) Plural nouns I've got *some* chocolates.	I haven't got *any* chocolates.	Have you got *any* chocolates?
b) uncountable nouns I need *some* money.	I don't need *any* money.	Do you need *any* money?
c) Singular nouns I'd like *a* cigarette.	I wouldn't like *a* cigarette.	Would you like *a* cigarette?
NOTE In questions where you expect the answer *yes*, we use *some* instead of *any*. *Example*: Could you give me *some* advice?		

The Smiths are going on holiday and are discussing what to take. Fill in the gaps in their conversation.

Mr Smith: I don't need (1) _____ sunglasses, but I'm taking (2) _____ books to read.

Mrs Smith: You don't need (3) _____ books. There won't be (4) _____ time to read. But don't forget to take (5) _____ shorts for the beach.

Mr Smith: I'll take my swimming costume.

Mrs Smith: You haven't got (6) _____ swimming costume.

Mr Smith: Oh yes. I must buy one. Can you give me (7) _____ money?

Mrs Smith: I haven't got (8) _____ money left. I bought (9) _____ new clothes this morning.

Mr Smith: More clothes? Haven't you got (10) _____ from last year?

Mrs Smith: Yes of course, but I needed (11) _____ sandals and (12) _____ sun dress.

Mr Smith: But you've got (13) _____ sun dress and (14) _____ sandals!

Mrs Smith: But they are last year's fashion.

Mr Smith: OK, OK. But have you put (15) _____ sports socks in for me? If I take my sandals, I'll need (16) _____ sports socks.

Mrs Smith: Yes, here you are. (17) _____ white ones and (18) _____ red ones.

Mr Smith: No blue ones?

Mrs Smith: You haven't got (19) _____ blue ones. Shall I buy (20) _____ ?

Mr Smith: No, don't bother. Two pairs are enough. There probably won't be (21) _____ sun while we are there.

26 Quantifiers: too/enough

too much work and not *enough* money

Example:

It's *very hot* in the summer. I like it.

It's *too hot* for me in the summer. I hate it!

(*Too* expresses a negative idea.)

Too and *enough* with adjectives:

Examples: (*too* + adjective) = (*not* + opposite adjective *enough*)
It's *too hot* for me in the summer. = It's *not cool enough* for me in the summer.
The car is *too expensive* for me. = The car is *not cheap enough* for me.

Exercise A

Complete the sentences, using *too . . .* or *not . . . enough* and one of the adjectives from the list below.

ADJECTIVES AND THEIR OPPOSITES:

hot	≠ cool / cold	dark	≠ light	poor	≠ rich
expensive	≠ cheap	high	≠ low	comfortable	≠ uncomfortable
far	≠ near	sweet	≠ sour	difficult	≠ easy

Example: The wall is not low enough for me to jump. The wall is *too high* for me to jump.

1 London isn't near enough for me to visit. London is _____ _____ for me to visit.

2 Martin isn't rich enough to buy a Rolls-Royce. Martin _____

3 This chair is too uncomfortable for me to sit on. This chair _____

4 These apples aren't sweet enough for me too eat. These apples _____

5 It's too dark to play football. It _____

6 This exercise isn't difficult enough! This exercise _____

Too and *enough* with *much* / *many* (see Unit 23):

Examples: (*too* + *much* + noun) (*not* + *enough* + noun)
There's *too much milk* in my tea. ≠ There's *not enough milk* in my tea.
There are *too many people* at the party. ≠ There are*n't enough people* at the party.

Exercise B

Complete the sentences, using *too much*, *too many* or *enough*.
Examples: He eats *too many* cakes. He doesn't eat *enough* fruit.

1 You drink _____ beer. 2 You don't drink _____ water.

3 She doesn't do _____ homework. 4 She spends _____ time watching television.

5 There are _____ children in the class. 6 There aren't _____ books for all of them.

7 England has _____ rain. 8 It doesn't get _____ sunshine.

ANSWERS

A 1 London is too far for me to visit. 2 Martin is too poor to buy a Rolls-Royce. 3 This chair isn't comfortable enough for me to sit on. 4 These apples are too sour for me to eat. 5 It isn't light enough to play football. 6 This exercise is too easy!

B 1 too much; 2 enough; 3 enough; 4 too much; 5 too many; 6 enough; 7 too much; 8 enough

---

When we ask a question, we normally put a verb *before* the subject.

Examples: Where *do* you live?   What *is* your name?   *Are* you happy?   *Is* it raining?

But when we ask an indirect question, we put the verb *after* the subject, as in a normal statement.

Examples: I would like to know where you *live*.   Can you tell me what your name *is*?
         Please tell me if you *are* happy.   Do you know if it *is* raining?

We often use indirect questions to be more polite.

Here are some opening phrases for indirect questions.

Can you tell me . . .   Do you know . . .
I would like to know . . .   Please could you tell me . . .
Could you tell me . . .

Exercise A

British police officers are usually friendly and happy to answer your questions.
But of course it is best to be polite!

Use the phrases given above to change these people's questions into indirect
questions.

What time is it?

1 Could _____

_____?

Where is the nearest post office?

2 Do _____

_____?

Are the pubs open?

3 Can _____

_____?

Is there a toilet near here?

4 Please _____

_____

How far is it to the station?

5 Could _____

_____?

When does the bank open?

6 I would _____

_____

Can I cross the road here?

7 Please _____

_____

When do the shops close?

8 Do you _____

_____?

Is this Oxford Street?

9 Can _____

_____?

Where can I buy some stamps?

10 I would _____

_____

Exercise B

Do Exercise 13 on the cassette.

28 Questions: wh–

What is this?

Wh- questions begin with question words like *What, When, Who, Whose, Why, Which, Where,* and *How*.

> What is your name?

QUESTION	ANSWER
What is your name? (verb) (subject)	My name is Maria. (subject) (verb)
Where are the children? (verb) (subject)	The children are in the garden. (subject) (verb)
When is she coming? (verb) (subject) (verb)	She is coming at 8 o'clock. (subject) (verb)
The verb comes *before* the subject.	**The verb comes *after* the subject.**

Exercise A

Write the questions.

1 What _____ ? His name is Juan.

2 Where _____ ? The pyramids are in Egypt.

3 Who _____ ? Alain was sick at the party.

4 Why _____ ? I am learning English because of my job.

5 How old _____ ? She is 20.

6 Whose car _____ ? It's my car.

PRESENT TENSE	PAST TENSE
a) Joan knows Mike. (subject) (verb) (object) Joan knows |who?| *Who* ◄ does Joan know? (object) (subject)	Joan knew Mike. (subject) (verb) (object) Joan knew |who?| *Who* ◄ did Joan know? (object) (subject)
b) Joan knows Mike. (subject) (verb) (object) |?| knows Mike? *Who* knows Mike? (subject) (verb) (object)	Joan knew Mike. (subject) (verb) (object) |?| knew Mike? *Who* knew Mike? (subject) (verb) (object)

Exercise B

Write the questions.

Examples: Who arrived at 7 o'clock? |?| arrived at 7 o'clock.
          Who did he see yesterday? He saw |?| yesterday.

1 Where _____ ? He went to |?| last week.

2 How many books _____ ? John bought |?| books last year.

3 Who _____ ? |?| bought a new car last month.

4 When _____ ? Phyllis went to China |?|

5 Which car _____ ? I like the |?| car.

6 What _____ ? |?| happened.

7 What _____ ? |?| You want ?

8 Whose pen _____ ? She took |?'s| pen.

29 Questions: yes/no

Are you a student?

Yes/no questions begin with a verb and expect the answer *yes* or *no*.

STATEMENT	QUESTION	SHORT ANSWER
You *are* English.	*Are* you English?	No, I'm not.
She *can* swim.	*Can* she swim?	Yes, she can.
It *is* raining.	*Is* it raining?	No, it isn't.
You *smoke*.	*Do* you smoke?	No, I don't.
They *will* help me.	*Will* they help me?	Yes, they will.
We *made* a mistake.	*Did* we make a mistake?	Yes, we did.

Exercise A

Change these statements into questions.

Examples: Rhona is studying law. ✓   *Is Rhona studying law? Yes, she is.*

Les went to Hong Kong last week. ✗   *Did Les go to Hong Kong last week? No, he didn't.*

1   Tony has gone to university. ✗   ?

2   Phyllis likes her new motorbike.? ✓   ?

3   Vanessa is going to work hard. ✓   ?

4   Robert will be two years old next week. ✗   ?

Exercise B

Write the questions.

Example: Meg / be / an artist? ✓   *Is Meg an artist? Yes, she is.*

1   Bill / like / fruit? ✗   ?

2   It / rain / yesterday? ✓   ?

3   you / watch TV / this evening? ✓   ?

4   Kerry / be born / in England? ✗   ?

5   Ben / play football / every Sunday? ✓   ?

30 Question tags

This is easy, *isn't it?*

Question tags are used to check information.

Your name is Tomoko, isn't it?

You come from Tokyo, don't you?

You haven't been to this school before, have you?

Yes, it is.

Yes, I do.

No, I haven't.

Positive statements with negative tags expect a positive answer.

POSITIVE STATEMENT	NEGATIVE TAG	EXPECTED ANSWER
It is raining,	isn't it?	Yes, it is.
You are Spanish,	aren't you?	Yes, I am.
She lives in London,	doesn't she?	Yes, she does.
He went to the disco,	didn't he?	Yes, he did.
You have a car,	don't you?	Yes, we do.

Negative statements with positive tags expect a negative answer.

NEGATIVE STATEMENT	POSITIVE TAG	EXPECTED ANSWER
It isn't raining,	is it?	No, it isn't.
You aren't Spanish,	are you?	No, I'm not.
She doesn't live in London,	does she?	No, she doesn't.
He didn't go to the disco,	did he?	No, he didn't.
You don't have a car,	do you?	No, we don't.

A police officer is checking information about a suspected thief. Write the tags.

1 You're Bill Grant, _____ _____ ?

2 You have a house in Priory Park, _____ _____ ?

3 Your wife's name is Meg, _____ _____ ?

4 You will be fifty next year, _____ _____ ?

5 You know this area well, _____ _____?

6 You don't like police officers,_____ _____ ?

7 You went to the pub last night,_____ _____ ?

8 You didn't go home last night, _____ _____ ?

9 You stole a white Renault car, _____ _____ ?

10 You're not telling the truth, _____ _____?

Do you think Bill Grant will give the expected answers every time?

ANSWERS
1 aren't you? 2 don't you?
3 isn't it? 4 won't you?
5 don't you? 6 do you?
7 didn't you? 8 did you?
9 didn't you? 10 are you?

31 Relative clauses: part A: subject.

I know a girl *who plays football.*

PEOPLE

I know a girl. *She* plays football.
   (Subject)

I know a girl *who plays football.*

A girl plays football. *She* lives near me.
   (Subject)

A girl *who lives near me* plays football.

THINGS

This is the key. *It* opens the door.
   (Subject)

This is the key *which opens the door.*

This is the key *that opens the door.*

The key is on the table. *It* opens the door.
   (Subject)

The key *which is on the table* opens the door.

The key *that is on the table* opens the door.

Join these sentences using *who, which* or *that*.
Example: The men are here. They want to talk to you. <u>*The men who want to talk to you are here.*</u>

1 The dog is in the garden. It is very dangerous.

  The dog _____ is very dangerous.

2 I want to meet the girls. They did this work.

  I want to _____ .

3 A person wanted to see me. Are you the person?

  Are you _____ ?

4 Somebody has just telephoned. He was interested in buying the car.

  Somebody _____

5 The train is on platform 4. It goes to Birmingham.

  The train _____

6 I am reading a book. It is about the life of Elvis Presley.

  I _____

7 We saw a boy. He was standing on his head.

  We _____

8 There is the house. It is for sale.

  There _____

ANSWERS **1** The dog that / which is in the garden is very dangerous. **2** I want to meet the girls who did this work. **3** Are you the person who wanted to see me? **4** Somebody who was interested in buying the car has just telephoned. **5** The train that/which goes to Birmingham is on platform 4 **6** I am reading a book that / which is about the life of Elvis Presley. **7** We saw a boy who was standing on his head. **8** There is the house that / which is for sale.

PEOPLE

This is the girl *I* met *her* today.
          (*Subject*)   (*Object*)

This is the girl *who I met today.*
This is the girl *that I met today.*
This is the girl *I met today.*

The girl plays football. *I* met *her* today.
          (*Subject*)   (*Object*)

The girl *who I met today* plays football.
The girl *that I met today* plays football.
The girl *I met today* plays football.

THINGS

This is the key. *I* found *it.*
    (*Subject*)   (*Object*)

This is the key *which I found.*
This is the key *that I found.*
This is the key *I found.*

The key opens the door. *I* found *it.*
        (*Subject*)   (*Object*)

The key *which I found* opens the door.
The key *that I found* opens the door.
The key *I found* opens the door.

Write a single sentence to join the two short sentences. If it is possible to do it without *who, which* or *that,* put the word in brackets ( ).

Example: Here are the books. You wanted them. <u>*Here are the books (which / that) you wanted.*</u>

1 Where are the apples? I bought them.

    Where are _____ ?

2 I am looking for the man. The police arrested him.

    I am looking _____ .

3 The book is missing. I bought it yesterday.

    The book _____ is missing.

4 The TV programme is at 8 o'clock. I like it.

    The TV programme _____ is at 8 o'clock.

5 This is a photograph of the man. I love him.

    This _____ .

6 The compact disc cost £12. I bought it.

    The compact disc _____ .

7 This is the bus. I have been waiting for it for half an hour.

    This _____ .

ANSWERS
1 Where are the apples (which / that) I bought? **2** I am looking for the man (who / that) the police arrested. **3** The book (which / that) I bought yesterday is missing. **4** The TV programme (which / that) I like is at 8 o'clock. **5** This is a photograph of the man (who / that) I love. **6** The compact disc (which / that) I bought cost £12. **7** This is the bus (which / that) I have been waiting for for half an hour.

'I like ice-cream.' 'So do I.'

I like ice-cream. / So do I.

I don't like fish. / Neither do I.

When someone makes a statement, you can agree by saying *So . . . I* or *Neither . . . I*
(verb)   (verb)

POSITIVE STATEMENT	AGREEMENT
I *am* hungry. I *was* here yesterday. I *live* in a city. He *lives* in Paris. We've *been* to Rome. She'*ll* be angry.	So *am* I. So *was* I. So *do* I. (NOT so *live* I.) So *does* she. So *have* they. So *will* he.

NEGATIVE STATEMENT	AGREEMENT
I'*m* not hungry. I *wasn't* here yesterday. I don't *live* in a city. He *doesn't live* in Paris. We *haven't been* to Rome. She *won't be* angry.	Neither *am* I. Neither *was* I. Neither *do* I. (Not Neither *live* I.) Neither *does* she. Neither *have* they. Neither *will* he.

When someone makes a statement, you can disagree by saying *(But) I . . . .*

POSITIVE STATEMENT	DISAGREEMENT
I *am* hungry. I *was* here yesterday. He *lives* in Paris. They'*ll* be angry.	I'*m not.* I *wasn't.* She *doesn't.* We *won't.*

NEGATIVE STATEMENT	DISAGREEMENT
I'*m not* hungry. I *wasn't* here yesterday. He *doesn't live* in Paris. They *won't be* angry.	I *am.* I *was.* He *does.* We *will.*

Exercise A

Mike makes a statement. Peter agrees, but David disagrees.

Example: I live in a big house.   *So do I.* ___   *But I don't.* ___
  My father has a big car.   *So has mine.* ___   *But mine hasn't.* ___

1   I can't swim.   a) _____   b) _____

2   I have two cats.   a) _____   b) _____

3   My sister has a big dog.   a) _____   b) _____

4   I'm nine years old.   a) _____   b) _____

5   I'll be ten next month.   a) _____   b) _____

6   I don't like girls.   a) _____   b) _____

7   My football is new.   a) _____   b) _____

8   I've cleaned my shoes.   a) _____   b) _____

9   I went to school today.   a) _____   b) _____

10   My mother doesn't smoke.   a) _____   b) _____

Exercise B

Do Exercise 14 on the cassette.

34 Verbs: conditional I

if . . .

Conditional I is used when things *usually* happen, or *are likely to* happen.

Exercise A

GENERAL CONDITIONS

Example: If you *put* milk into the fridge, it *stays* cold.
        (*present simple*)   (*present simple*)

or: Milk *stays* cold if you *put* it into the fridge.

Choose the correct endings.

1 Water boils if _____

2 If I am late for work, _____

3 My teacher gets angry if _____

4 If I feel tired, _____

5 I don't like driving if _____

6 If the weather is cold, _____

my boss gets very angry
I always wear a coat
I don't do my homework
the roads are busy
you heat it to 100°C
I usually go to bed early

Exercise B

LIKELY CONDITIONS

Example: You *will catch* the bus if you *hurry*.
          (*future*)   (*present tense*)

or: If you *hurry*,   you *will catch* the bus.
          (*present simple*)   (*future*)

Choose the correct endings.

1 If it rains, _____

2 My teacher will be pleased if _____

3 If I study hard, _____

4 I'll be disappointed if _____

5 If you're not busy this evening, _____

6 The boys will play football _____

I do my homework tonight
will you come to the party?
I won't go for a walk
if they have time
I don't pass my exams
my English will improve

35 Verbs: conditional II

if I were you . . .

Conditional II is used for imaginary situations, or situations which are not likely to happen.

Examples:

If I   *met*   a rich young man, I   *would marry*   him.
        (*past simple*)   (*would + verb*)
If I   *married*   him,   I   *would buy*   a lot of clothes.
(or: I *would buy*   a lot of clothes if I   *married*   him.

Exercise A

Complete the following sentences.

1 If he ——————— harder, he ——————— the exam.
        (*work*)   (*pass*)

2 She ——————— to America if she ——————— enough money.
        (*go*)   (*have*)

3 If England ——————— better weather, more tourists ——————— to visit.
            (*have*)   (*come*)

Conditional II is also used for giving advice.
Example:

"If I *were* you, *I'd*
sell that car!"

If	I / we / you he / she / it / they	were. . .

NB: In spoken English,
some people say
I was, he was or
she was.

Exercise B

Give advice to these people.

1 ——————— , ——————— (*eat less*)

2 ——————— , ——————— (*stop smoking*)

3 ——————— , ——————— (*go to the dentist*)

Verbs: future with going to

I *am going to* sing.

STATEMENT		
I	am / 'm / am not / 'm not	
You / We / They	are / 're / are not / aren't	going to sing.
He / She / It	is / 's / is not / isn't	

QUESTION		
Am / Aren't	I	
Are / Aren't	you / we / they	going to sing?
Is / Isn't	he / she / it	

SHORT ANSWER		
Yes, / No,	I	am. / 'm not.
Yes, / No,	you / we / they	are. / aren't.
Yes, / No,	he / she / it	is. / isn't.

We use *going to* when we know what is going to happen, or we think the other person knows what is going to happen.

Examples:

What *are you going to do*?

I'm *going to play* the piano.

Is he going to play the drums?

No, he isn't. He's going to play the piano.

Exercise A

What is going to happen?

1   She / read / a book   _____

2   They / watch / TV   _____

3   He / not play / the drums   _____

4   She / not do / her homework   _____

5   I / do / my homework   _____

6   You / do / your homework?   _____

7   It / rain   _____

8   It / not / rain   _____

9   It / rain?   _____

10   They / not come / to the party   _____

Exercise B

Do Exercise 15 on the cassette.

ANSWERS
A 1 She is going to read a book. 2 They are going to watch TV. 3 He is not going to play the drums. 4 She is not going to do her homework. 5 I am going to do my homework. 6 Are you going to do your homework? 7 It is going to rain. 8 It isn't going to rain. 9 Is it going to rain? 10 They are not going to come to the party.

STATEMENT		
I	am 'm am not 'm not	
You We They	are 're are not aren't	coming.
He She It	is 's is not isn't	

QUESTION		
Am Aren't	I	
Are Aren't	you we they	coming?
Is Isn't	he she it	

SHORT ANSWER		
Yes, No,	I	am. 'm not.
Yes, No,	you we they	are. aren't.
Yes, No,	he she it	is. isn't.

We use the *present continuous* to talk about the future when we have plans or arrangements.

Examples:

Sorry, *I'm playing tennis on Monday, but I'm not doing* anything on Tuesday.

I'm having tea with my cousin on Tuesday. What *are you doing* on Wednesday?

Write about the following plans.

1 She / see / the bank manager at 3 o'clock. _____

2 He / have dinner / at 8.30 pm. _____

3 You / fly / to Paris / tomorrow? _____

4 What time / they / leave London? _____

5 We / not play / golf / on Sunday. _____

6 She / have / a party / next Saturday. _____

7 I / meet / my girlfriend / at the cinema. _____

8 He / not come / to tea / tomorrow. _____

9 The new supermarket / open / on 28th June. _____

10 I / not go / to the dentist / until next year. _____

The plane *leaves* at 6 o'clock.

STATEMENT	
I You We They	leave. don't leave.
He She It	leaves. doesn't leave.

QUESTION		
Do Don't	I you we they	leave?
Does Doesn't	he she it	

SHORT ANSWER		
Yes, No,	I you we they	do. don't.
Yes, No,	he she it	does. doesn't.

We use the *present simple* for the future when we talk about timetables, programmes and schedules.
Example:

We leave tomorrow morning.

What time?

Anne and Mary have booked a holiday in Europe. Anne is telling her parents about it.
Complete the conversation.

Mr Smith: What time _____ the plane _____ _____? (*take off*)

Anne: It _____ _____ at 9.30 am and _____ (*land*) in Paris at 10.30.

Mr Smith: How many days _____ you _____ in Paris? (*spend*)

Anne: Two. We're staying in a hotel on the Champs Elysées. Then on Monday morning we _____ a train to Marseilles. (*take*)

Mrs Smith: How long _____ that journey _____? (*take*)

Anne: Only four hours. We _____ at 2.30 pm. (*arrive*)

Mrs Smith: What about your lunch?

Anne: We'll buy some sandwiches. The ticket _____ _____ _____ food. (*not include*)

Mr Smith: How long _____ you _____ in Marseilles? (*have*)

Anne: Four days. But we _____ on day trips to Nice and St Tropez. (*go*)

Mrs Smith: How lovely!

39 Verbs: future with time clauses

I'll tell him when I see him.

These conjunctions can be used to refer to the future, but they are followed by a verb in the present tense.

when	I'll tell him *when* I see him. / *When* I see him, I'll tell him.
as soon as	We'll start *as soon as* he comes. / *As soon as* he comes, we'll start.
before	He'll phone *before* he leaves. / *Before* he leaves, he'll phone.
by the time	It'll be dark *by the time* they arrive. / *By the time* they arrive, it'll be dark.
the moment	They'll do it *the moment* they get here. / *The moment* they get here, they'll do it.
until	She'll stay *until* it ends. (Don't start with *until*)

Exercise A

We'll start as soon as he goes to sleep.

Link the two halves of the following sentences.

1 We'll go for a walk   until the fog clears.
2 When the summer comes,   the teacher will tell us the answer.
3 The terrorist will be arrested   as soon as it stops raining.
4 The plane won't take off   it'll be much warmer.
5 Before he ends the class,   the moment he enters the country.

Exercise B

In the following sentences, choose the correct pairs of verbs from the list below and put them in the correct tense.

1 My mother _____ very pleased when I _____ her.

2 As soon as I _____ school, I _____ the army.

3 The meeting _____ until they _____ agreement.

4 By the time they _____ here, we _____ ready for them.

5 The boss _____ before the shop _____ .

get/be	leave/join	return/close	continue/reach	be/visit

ANSWERS

A 1 We'll go for a walk as soon as it stops raining. **2** When the summer comes, it'll be much warmer. **3** The terrorist will be arrested the moment he enters the country. **4** The plane won't take off until the fog clears. **5** Before he ends the class, the teacher will tell us the answer.

B 1 My mother *will be* very pleased when I *visit* her. **2** As soon as I *leave* school, I'll *join* the army. **3** The meeting *will continue* until they *reach* agreement. **4** By the time they *get* here, *we'll be* ready for them. **5** The boss *will return* before the shop *closes*.

I'll go . . .

STATEMENT		
I You We They He She It	will 'll won't	come.

QUESTION		
Will	I you we they he she it	come?

SHORT ANSWER			
Yes, No,	I you we they he she it	will. won't.

We use the future with *will* to express the following.

PREDICTION

In Scotland it will rain tomorrow. In the south of England it will be sunny.

QUICK DECISION

I'll have steak.

I think I'll have fish.

PROMISE

I'll phone you again tomorrow.

Example:

I think I / stay / in bed tomorrow.   *I think I'll stay in bed tomorrow.*

1   I don't think she / go / to the party.

2   The weather / be / sunny in June.

3   You / help / me?

4   There / not be / enough water next summer.

5   I think I / go / to the bank.

6   He / pay / you tomorrow.

7   I / have / soup, please.

8   The government says we / have / more money next year.

9   You / marry / me?

10 No, I / not lend / you any money.

41 Verbs: future review

talking about the future

In English there is no one special tense to talk about the future. The tense we use depends on the situation. Look at Worksheets 36 to 40 and complete the following.

1 The car is dirty!

I'm not _____ _____ wash the car,

I'm _____ _____ clean the windows.

2 I've got a headache.

I _____ get an aspirin for you.

3 Let's tidy this room.

My parents _____ (come) at 8 o'clock.

What time _____ their train _____ (arrive)

4 What would you like to drink?

I _____ have a cup of tea, please.

5

We _____ (not be) back late.

The film _____ (finish) at 10 o'clock.

6 Did you feed the cat?

No. I _____ do it now.

7

Look at those clouds. It _____ to rain.

8

We must come here tomorrow. The Scroggs _____ (play).

9

_____ he _____ _____ paint the room that colour?

10

I _____ _____ (be) thirty next year!

42 Verbs: gerunds and infinitives

I enjoy *studying*. He offered *to help*.

He *likes* play*ing* football.   She *enjoys* danc*ing*.   He *loves* cycl*ing*.

They *dislike* jogg*ing*.   We *hate* writ*ing* letters.   I don't *enjoy* read*ing* magazines.

The teacher doesn't *like* mark*ing* homework.

Exercise A

Write a sentence for each of the pictures. Choose a verb from the list below:

cook / swim / play tennis / write letters / play the piano / sing / watch TV

JOHN (*like*)   MARY (*enjoy*)   SUE (*like*)   AHMED (*hate*)

Example:
John likes fishing.   1 _____   2 _____   3 _____

NINA (*not enjoy*)   SVEN (*love*)   YOKO (*not like*)   DAVID (*dislike*)

4 _____   5 _____   6 _____   7 _____

Some other verbs also have an *-ing* verb following them: stop / start / keep / deny + *-ing*

BUT: the following verbs take *to* + infinitive: want / promise / learn / expect / offer.

Exercise B

Use the verb given to complete the sentence, with either *to* + infinitive or *-ing* (gerund).

Example: Where did you learn <u>to do</u> that? (*do*)

1   You must stop _____ . It's bad for you.   (*smoke*)

2   When do you expect _____ your new car?   (*get*)

3   My boyfriend keeps _____ me to marry him.   (*ask*)

4   He has offered _____ his sister with her work.   (*help*)

5   My husband promised _____ the meal this evening.   (*cook*)

6   The thief denied _____ the old lady's handbag.   (*steal*)

7   Nobody wants _____ this exercise.   (*do*)

8   The orchestra started _____ when they walked in.   (*play*)

Andy and Audrey Jackson: Elementary Grammar Worksheets Photocopy Masters © Prentice Hall International (UK) Ltd 1992. All rights reserved

43 Verbs: have got
I've got . . .

STATEMENT		
I You We They	have 've have not haven't	got. . .
He She It	has 's has has not hasn't	

QUESTION		
Have	I you we they	got. . .?
Has	he she it	

SHORT ANSWER		
Yes, No,	I you we they	have. haven't.
Yes, No,	he she it	has. hasn't.

Examples:
Has he got a ticket?
    Yes, he has.

Have they got a car?

No, they haven't.

I've got a headache.

Have you?

Exercise A

Write out the following sentences in full.

Example: Mr and Mrs Smith / not got / a car.   *Mr and Mrs Smith haven't got a car.*

1 How much money / Anne / got?   _____

2 What / you / got / in your hand?   _____

3 My sister / got / three cats.   _____

4 We / not got / much time.   _____

5 You / got / change for £5?   _____

6 Our friends / not got / a big house.   _____

Have got means the same as *have*.

STATEMENT	
I You We They	have 've do not have don't have
He She It	's has doesn't have

QUESTION		
Do	I you we they	have. . .?
Does	he she it	

SHORT ANSWER		
Yes, No,	I you we they	do. don't.
Yes, No,	he she it	does. doesn't.

Exercise B

Write the first four sentences again, using *have* instead of *have got*.
Example: Mr and Mrs Smith / not have / a car   *Mr and Mrs Smith don't have a car.*

1 _____   2 _____

3 _____   4 _____

44 Verbs: like or would like?

I *like* dancing. I*'d like* to dance.

We use *like* to talk about general things.
It can be followed by a noun: I *like* pop music.
or a verb with *-ing*:   I *like* dancing.

We use *would like* (*'d like*) to talk about things we want now.
It can be followed by a noun: I *would (I'd) like* a cup of coffee.
or a verb with *to*:   I *would (I'd) like* to dance.

Exercise A

Fill in the gaps in these sentences with *like(s)* or *would like*.

1   I _____ to stay longer, but I must go home now.

2   John _____ football. He plays every week.

3   Maria _____ to speak to you.

4   Who _____ another drink?

5   Most English people _____ tea in the afternoon.

Exercise B

Put the verb in the correct form (*to . . .* or *-ing*) in the following sentences:

1   My husband doesn't like _____ to the cinema. He prefers TV.   (*go*)

2   I would like _____ you but I'm rather busy.   (*help*)

3   I don't like _____ early on Sunday mornings.   (*get up*)

4   This government would like _____ taxes.   (*raise*)

5   Would you like _____ to my party?   (*come*)

45 Verbs: modal auxiliaries can/could

I can, I could. . .

STATEMENT			QUESTION			SHORT ANSWER		
I You We They He She It	can can't	swim.	Can Can't	I you we they he she it	swim?	Yes, No,	I you we they he she it	can. can't.

Can = I know how to do it, or it is possible for me to do it.

Example: Can you swim? Yes, I can. Can you ski? No, I can't. You can't dive in here.

Exercise A

Write statements with *can* or *can't*.

1 They _____ dance. **2** He _____ ski. **3** _____ drive.

Exercise B

The *past tense* of *can / can't* is *could / couldn't*. Complete these sentences.

1 Last year they _____ **2** Last year he _____ **3** Last year she _____

dance.

We also use *can* or *could* for making requests. (*Could* is very polite.)
Example:

Exercise C

Write requests using *can* or *could*.

1 You want to read someone's newspaper. _____

2 You want a friend to post a letter for you. _____

3 You want someone to pass the salt. _____

4 You want to watch TV. _____

STATEMENT		
I You We They	have to don't have to	go. come
He She It	has to doesn't have to	work.
I You We They	have got to 've got to haven't to	go. come
He She It	has got to 's got to hasn't got to	work.

QUESTION			
Do Don't	I you we they	have to	go? come?
Does Doesn't	he she it		work?
Have Haven't	I you we they	got to	go? come?
Has Hasn't	he she it		work?

SHORT ANSWER		
Yes, No,	I you we they	do. don't.
Yes, No,	he she it	does. doesn't.
Yes, No,	I you we they	have. haven't
Yes, No,	he she it	has. hasn't.

Have got to and *have to* mean it is necessary, usually because of another authority. The negatives (*don't have to / haven't got it*) mean it is not necessary. (See Worksheet 48 on *must / mustn't*).

Exercise A

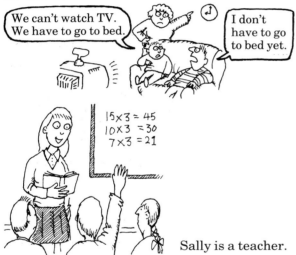

We can't watch TV. We have to go to bed.

I don't have to go to bed yet.

No, I can't go out. I've got to do my homework.

Do you *have* to do it?

Sally is a teacher.

John is a shop assistant.

What do they have to do?

Example: <u>*Sally has to go to university.*</u> ✓ go to university ✗ <u>*John doesn't have to go to university.*</u>

1 _____ ✗ work on Saturdays ✓ _____
2 _____ ✓ mark homework ✗ _____
3 _____ ✓ write reports ✗ _____
4 _____ ✗ serve customers ✓ _____
5 _____ ✗ take money ✓ _____

 Exercise B

Do Exercise 16 on the cassette.

47 Verbs: modal auxiliaries with may/might

We *may* do that.

I/You We/They He/She/It	may (not) might (not)	go. come. work.

We use *may* or *might* when we think something is possible.
May is often more possible than *might*.

Examples: What are you going to do this afternoon? We don't know yet. We *may* watch a video.
We *might* not like this video. No, this one *might* be better.

Exercise A

Write sentences with *may* (*not*) and *might* (*not*) for the following situations.

1 BE SUNNY?

RAIN?

a) It _____

b) _____

2 GO BY BUS?

GO BY TAXI?

a) They _____

b) _____

3 PEACE IN THE WORLD?

ANOTHER WAR?

a) There _____

b) _____

4 DO MY HOMEWORK?

GO TO THE CINEMA?

a) She _____

b) _____

Exercise B

May I . . .? means *Is it OK if I . . .?*
Example: May I use your pen? Yes, here you are.
Ask:

1 You want to read someone's newspaper. _____ ?

2 You want to open a window. _____ ?

3 You want to turn on the TV. _____ ?

We *must* do this.

I You We They He She It	must must not mustn't	go. work. be...

I You We They	don't need to need not needn't	go. work. be...
He She It	doesn't need to need not needn't	

Must or *mustn't* means it <u>is</u> necessary.   *Needn't* means it is <u>not</u> necessary.

Authority:

You *must* drive on the left in England.   You *must* take this medicine.   You *mustn't* walk on the grass.
You *must not* drive on the right.   You *needn't* stay in bed.   You *needn't* go home yet.

Exercise A

Use *must / mustn't / needn't*.

1

You _____ _____

_____ _____ when you go to England.

2

You _____ be late for school.

3

You _____ change your English money
when you go to Scotland.

4

You _____ smoke in the classroom.

Personal opinion:

Examples: We *must* hurry or we'll be late.   I *mustn't* make any mistakes.
   You *needn't* clean the window. I did it yesterday.

Exercise B

Use *must / mustn't / needn't*.

1

You _____ take an umbrella.

2

I _____ go to the bank.

3

I _____ be late.

49 Verbs: modal auxiliaries with should

We *should* do that.

I/You We/They He/She/It	should should not shouldn't	go. come. work.

We use *should* when it is a <u>good</u> thing to do.
We also use it to give advice.
We use *should not* or *shouldn't* when it is a <u>bad</u> thing to do.

Examples: You *shouldn't* bite your finger nails! You *should* study hard and go to university.

Exercise A

Change these orders into advice.

Examples: Write to your mother!   *You should write to your mother.*

Don't put your feet on the table!   *You shouldn't put your feet on the table.*

1   It's a nice day. Don't stay in the house! _____

2   Go for a walk!   _____

3   Visit your aunt!   _____

4   Respect older people!   _____

5   Don't watch TV all day!   _____

Exercise B

Now use *should* or *shouldn't* to give advice to these people.

1 She _____ eat so much.   2 He _____ _____ .   3 He _____ _____ to the dentist.

4 She _____ _____   5 They _____ _____   6 He _____ _____

to the police.   _____ _____ .   his car.

STATEMENT		
I	was was not wasn't	understood. (*past participle*)
You We They	were were not weren't	
He She It	was was not wasn't	

QUESTION		
Was	I	understood? (*past participle*)
Were	you we they	
Was	he she it	

SHORT ANSWER		
Yes, No,	I	was. was not. wasn't.
	you we they	were. were not. weren't.
	he she it	was. was not. wasn't.

The *passive tense* is used:

a) if the subject is not known.

Example: *Someone* stole *my bicycle* yesterday. (*ACTIVE*)
        (*subject*)   (*object*)

My bicycle was stolen yesterday.   (*PASSIVE*)

or **b**) if the object is more important than the subject.

Example: Fire destroyed *the Smiths' house* last week. (*ACTIVE*)
               (*object*)

The Smiths' house *was destroyed* by fire last week. (*PASSIVE*)

Exercise A

Change these sentences from active to passive.

1 Bombs killed many people during the war. _____

2 Someone made this car in Japan. _____

3 The gardener didn't cut the grass this morning. _____

4 The teacher didn't correct the exam papers last night. _____

5 Did someone invite the Queen to the wedding? _____

Exercise B

Do Exercise 17 on the cassette.

51 Verbs: passive, present simple

We are understood.

STATEMENT		
I	am 'm am not	
You We They	are 're are not aren't	understood. (*past participle*)
He She It	is 's 's not isn't	

QUESTION		
Am	I	
Are	you we they	understood? (*past participle*)
Is	he she it	

SHORT ANSWER		
Yes, No,	I	am. am not.
Yes, No,	you we they	are. aren't.
Yes, No,	he she it	is. isn't.

The *passive tense* is used:

a) if the subject is not known:

Example: *Someone* repairs *my car* in that garage. (*ACTIVE*)
(*subject*)   (*object*)

My car *is repaired* in that garage.   (*PASSIVE*)

or **b**) if the object is more important than the subject:

Example: Every year the manager invites *the prince*
to the exhibition.   (*object*)   (*ACTIVE*)

Every year the prince *is invited* to the exhibition
(by the manager).   (PASSIVE)

Change these sentences from active to passive.

1   People speak English all over the world.   _____

2   Does the gardener water the flowers every day?   _____

3   I'm sorry but we don't accept credit cards here.   _____

4   People grow coffee in Brazil.   _____

5   Does the teacher allow smoking in the classroom? _____

ANSWERS
1 English is spoken all over the world. 2 Are the flowers watered every day? 3 I'm sorry but credit cards aren't accepted here. 4 Coffee is grown in Brazil. 5 Is smoking allowed in the classroom?

52 Verbs: past continuous

I was sleeping.

STATEMENT		
I	was wasn't	
You We They	were weren't	reading.
He She It	was wasn't	

QUESTION		
Was Wasn't	I	
Were Weren't	you we they	reading?
Was Wasn't	he she it	

SHORT ANSWER			
Yes, No,	I	was. wasn't.
	you we they	were. weren't.
	he she it	was. wasn't.

We use the *past continuous tense* to describe what was happening at a particular time.

Saturday afternoon

The dog was chasing the cat.

Mrs Smith was cleaning the bedroom.

Mr Smith was washing the dishes.

The children were watching TV.

Saturday night

Mr and Mrs Smith were sleeping.

The children were sleeping.

The cat was chasing a mouse.

The dog was lying on the floor.

Look at the picture and answer the following questions.

Example: What was the dog doing at 3 pm?   *It was chasing the cat.*

1 What was Mrs Smith doing at 3 pm?   _____

2 Was Mr Smith sleeping at 3 pm?   _____

3 Where was the dog lying at 3 am?   _____

4 What was the cat doing at 3 am?   _____

5 Were the children sleeping at 3 am?   _____

6 What were Mr and Mrs Smith doing at 3 am?   _____

7 Was the cat sleeping at 3 am?   _____

8 What were the children doing at 3 pm?   _____

9 Was the cat chasing the dog at 3 pm?   _____

10 What was Mrs Smith cleaning?   _____

Andy and Audrey Jackson: Elementary Grammar Worksheets Photocopy Masters © Prentice Hall International (UK) Ltd 1992. All rights reserved

53

Verbs: past habitual

I *used to play* football.

1957

Now

She used to dance, but now she plays golf.

1972

Now

He used to play football but now he likes to watch it.

We used to do something regularly in the past, but we don't do it now.

Exercise A

Look at these pictures and write a sentence about each, using the words given.

ride a motorbike / but now / drive a car

1 John _____

play tennis / but now / read books

2 Mary _____

work in a bank / but now / teach

3 She _____

live in Paris / but now / live in Rome

4 I _____

be very slim / but now / eat too much

5 He _____

smoke heavily / but now / go jogging

6 They _____

Exercise B

Do Exercise 18 on the cassette.

54

Verbs: past simple with irregular verbs

I *came*, he *went*.

STATEMENT		NEGATIVE			QUESTION			SHORT ANSWER		
I	got up. woke up. had... went. drank. ate. left. came. read. wrote.	I		get up. wake up. have... go. drink. eat. leave. come. read. write.		I	get up? wake up? have? go? drink? eat? leave? come? read? write?		I	did.
You We		You We	didn't		Did Didn't	we they		Yes, No, didn't.	you we they	
They		They								
He She It		He She It				he she it			he she it	

7:00	Mr and Mrs Smith got up.
8:00	The children got up.
8:30	Mr Smith had his breakfast and then drove to work.
8:45	The children ran to school. They didn't go by car.
9:00	Mrs Smith went to work.
10:30	Mr Smith drank a cup of coffee. The children didn't drink anything.
12:00	Mr Smith ate his sandwiches at the office.

4:00	Mrs Smith came home.
4:00	The children left school.
6:00	The Smith family had dinner.
9:00	The children went to bed.
10:00	Mr Smith read the newspaper.
10:00	Mrs Smith wrote a letter.
11:00	Mr and Mrs Smith went to bed.

What did the Smith family do today? Fill in the blanks.

Mr Smith: I _____ _____ at 7 o'clock and _____ my breakfast at 8.30 and then _____ to work. At 10.30 I _____ a cup of coffee. At 12 o'clock _____ _____ my sandwiches. In the evening I _____ my newspaper and _____ _____ to bed at 11.

My wife _____ _____ at 7 o'clock and at 9 o'clock _____ _____ to work. She _____ _____ at 4 o'clock and at 6 o'clock we _____ dinner. _____ _____ a letter at 10 o'clock and _____ to bed at the same time as me. The children _____ _____ at 8 o'clock. They _____ to school at 8.45. _____ didn't _____ by car. They _____ school at 4 and _____ dinner with us at 6 o'clock. Then at 9 o'clock _____ _____ to bed.

ANSWERS
Mr Smith: I *got up* at 7 o'clock and *had* my breakfast at 8.30 and then I *drove* to work. At 10.30 I *drank* a cup of coffee. At 12 o'clock I *ate* my sandwiches. In the evening I *read* my newspaper and I *went* to bed at 11. My wife *got up* at 7 o'clock and at 9 o'clock she *went* to work. She *came* home at 4 o'clock and at 6 o'clock we *had* dinner. *She wrote* a letter at 10 o'clock and went to bed at the same time as me. The children *got up* at 8 o'clock. They *ran* to school at 8.45. *They didn't go* by car. They *left* school at 4 and *had* dinner with us at 6 o'clock. Then at 9 o'clock *they went* to bed.

I *listened*, he *talked*.

STATEMENT	
I You We They He She It	listen*ed*. didn't listen.

QUESTION		
Did Didn't	I you we they he she it	listen?

SHORT ANSWER		
Yes, No,	I you we they he she it	did. didn't

The *past simple tense* is used for regular actions in the past, or single actions.

What did the Smith family do yesterday?

 At 8.15 the children washed their hands and faces.

At 9 o'clock Mr Smith arrived at the office.

 At 10 o'clock the children played with their friends.

At 12.30 Mr Smith walked to the pub for lunch. He didn't stay in the office.

At 3.30 the children finished school.

At 7 o'clock Mr Smith cleaned the car.

At 8.30 the children cleaned their teeth. They didn't brush their hair.

At 10 o'clock Mr Smith talked to his wife.

Exercise A

Mrs Smith worked at the hospital all day. When she arrived home she asked the family some questions.

Fill in the blanks in the conversations below.

1 _____ you _____ your hands and faces this morning?

Yes, _____ _____

2 What _____ you do at school?

We _____ with our friends.

3 _____ you _____ in the office for lunch?

No, I _____

I _____ to the pub.

4 Who _____ the car?

_____

5 _____ the children _____ their teeth and _____ their hair?

They _____ their teeth but _____ their hair.

Exercise B

Do Exercise 19 on the cassette.

56 Verbs: past simple or past continuous?

I *was reading* when she *came*.

We use the *past simple tense* for completed actions.
We use the *past continuous tense* for actions which weren't completed.

When he *got up*,
the sun *was shining*.

While he *was eating* breakfast
the phone *rang*. He *got up* and
answered it.

While they *were playing*
football it *began* to rain.

Make complete sentences for the following pictures.

1 Jack / walk / down the street / when / see / an accident. He / go / to a phone box / and / call / the police.

_____

2 While Mr and Mrs Smith / watch / TV, a burglar / come / into the room / and / steal / their money.

_____

3 John / work / in his room / when / hear / a noise. He / go / outside / and / see / his dog. It / chase / a cat.

_____

_____

Andy and Audrey Jackson: Elementary Grammar Worksheets Photocopy Masters © Prentice Hall International (UK) Ltd 1992. All rights reserved

A phrasal verb is a verb + preposition(s) where the preposition(s) changes the meaning of the original verb.

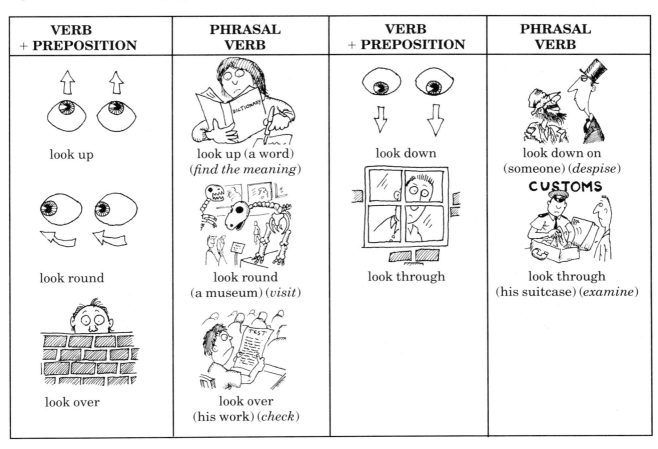

VERB + PREPOSITION	PHRASAL VERB	VERB + PREPOSITION	PHRASAL VERB
look up	look up (a word) (*find the meaning*)	look down	look down on (someone) (*despise*)
look round	look round (a museum) (*visit*)	look through	look through (his suitcase) (*examine*)
look over	look over (his work) (*check*)		

More phrasal verbs with *look*

look after (*take care of*)

look for (*try to find*)

look forward to (*expect with pleasure*)

Complete these sentences with one of the phrasal verbs above.

1   The policeman _____ _____ the thief's bag.

2   If you don't know the word you must _____ it _____ in the dictionary.

3   Mary _____ _____ our dog when we went on holiday.

4   You should not _____ _____ _____ people who are less intelligent than you.

5   Have you seen my pen? I've _____ _____ it everywhere.

6   Would you like to _____ _____ our new house?

7   I'm _____ _____ _____ the summer holidays.

8   Now you should _____ _____ these sentences to find any mistakes.

58

Verbs: phrasal verbs II: put. . .

Put it out!

The verb *put* in its original meaning, needs a preposition or particle to tell us where.
We never use *put* on its own, and we can ask a question with *where*?.

Sometimes the preposition or particle can change the meaning of the original
verb. Then we cannot ask the question *where*?
There is sometimes another single verb with the same meaning.

Exercise A

Use the dictionary to find the meaning of the words on the right, and then link
them to the correct sentence.

1   The firemen *put* the fire *out* with water.   *(kill)*

2   They had to *put off* the football match because it was raining.   *(increase)*

3   I am *putting aside* a little every month for my holiday.   *(extinguish)*

4   The horse was so badly injured that they had to *put it down*.   *(postpone)*

5   When I stopped smoking I started to *put on* weight.   *(save)*

Exercise B

Choose one of the phrasal verbs in Exercise A to complete each of these sentences.

1   The dog was very old, so John had it _____ _____ .

2   This dress is very tight. I have _____ _____ at least three kilos.

3   If you can do it today, don't _____ it _____ until tomorrow.

4   Never try to _____ an electrical fire _____ with water.

5   He is _____ _____ 10% of his salary for a pension.

59

Verbs: phrasal verbs III: General

Look after the children.

Look at these phrasal verbs.

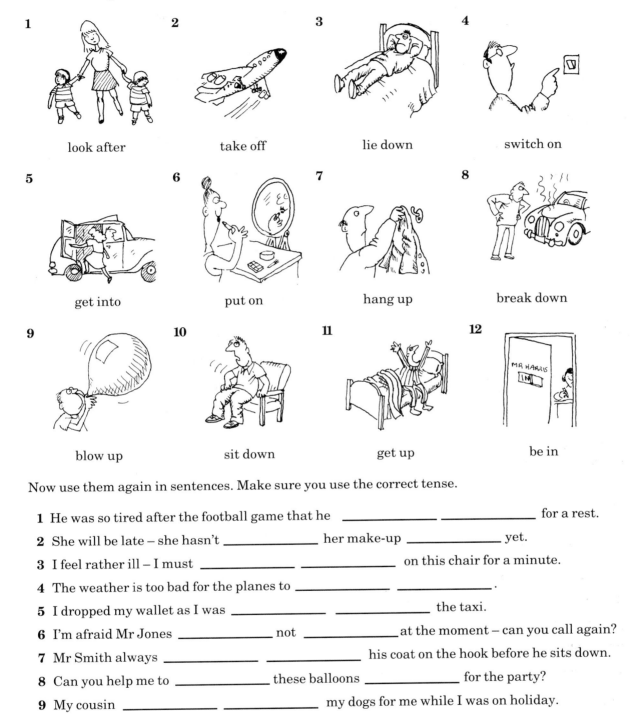

1 look after

2 take off

3 lie down

4 switch on

5 get into

6 put on

7 hang up

8 break down

9 blow up

10 sit down

11 get up

12 be in

Now use them again in sentences. Make sure you use the correct tense.

1 He was so tired after the football game that he _____ _____ for a rest.

2 She will be late – she hasn't _____ her make-up _____ yet.

3 I feel rather ill – I must _____ _____ on this chair for a minute.

4 The weather is too bad for the planes to _____ _____ .

5 I dropped my wallet as I was _____ _____ the taxi.

6 I'm afraid Mr Jones _____ not _____ at the moment – can you call again?

7 Mr Smith always _____ _____ his coat on the hook before he sits down.

8 Can you help me to _____ these balloons _____ for the party?

9 My cousin _____ _____ my dogs for me while I was on holiday.

10 My car has _____ _____ five times this winter.

11 I never enjoy _____ _____ very early in the morning.

12 Quick – _____ the radio _____ . I want to hear the news!

60 Verbs: present continuous

I am going.

STATEMENT		
I	am 'm 'm not	
You We They	are 're are not 're not	going.
He She It	is 's is not isn't 's not	

QUESTION		
Am	I	
Are	you we they	going?
Is	he she it	

SHORT ANSWER		
Yes,	I	am. 'm not.
	you we they	are. aren't.
No,	he she it	is. isn't.

The *present continuous tense* talks about what is happening now.

Look at the picture. It's 3 o'clock on Sunday afternoon.

The dog is chasing the cat.   The children are playing with a ball.   The fish is swimming.   Grandad is sleeping.

Examples: What is the fish doing?   *It's swimming.*
              Is the fish swimming?   *Yes, it is.*

1   What is Mrs Smith doing?   _____

2   Is Grandad reading?   _____

3   What is the cat doing?   _____

4   Is the dog sleeping?   _____

5   What are the children playing with?   _____

6   What is the dog doing?   _____

7   What is Mr Smith doing?   _____

8   Are Mrs Smith and Grandad working?   _____

9   Is Mr Smith working?   _____

10   Are you working?!   _____

ANSWERS
1 She's reading. **2** No, he isn't. **3** It's hiding in the tree. **4** No, it isn't. **5** They're playing with a ball. **6** It's chasing a cat. **7** He's cutting the grass. **8** No, they aren't. **9** Yes, he is. **10** Yes, I am!

STATEMENT			QUESTION			SHORT ANSWER		
I You We They	have 've have not haven't	been working.	Have	I you we they	been working?	Yes, No,	I you we they	have. haven't.
He She It	has 's has not hasn't		Has	he she it		Yes, No,	he she it	has. hasn't.

The *present perfect continuous tense* looks in the present at an action which started in the past and may have finished or may be continuing.

Why is she crying?
She's been chopping onions.

I'm tired. *I've been painting* this room all day.

They're fed up. *They've been waiting* for the bus.

Exercise A

Why is the Smith family tired?

1

Mr Smith _____ _____ _____. (*drive*)

4

The dog _____ _____ _____. (*chase*) the cat.

2

Mrs Smith _____ _____ _____. (*garden*)

5

Grandma and Grandpa _____ _____ _____.
(*walk*) in the park.

3

The children _____ _____ _____. (*play*) football.

Exercise B

Do Exercise 20 on the cassette.

62 Verbs: present perfect simple

I *have* seen. . .

STATEMENT		
I You We They	have 've have not haven't	seen. . . (*past participle*)
He She It	has 's has not hasn't	

QUESTION		
Have	I you we they	seen. . .? (*past participle*)
Has	he she it	

SHORT ANSWER		
Yes, No,	I you we they	have. haven't.
	he she it	has. hasn't.

The *present perfect* tense looks in the present at actions completed in the past.

He's *cleaned* the car.

She's *finished* her homework.

They've *eaten* a Chinese meal.

Fill in the blanks.

1 What have they done?

_____ _____ a film. (*see*)

2 What _____ he done?

_____ _____ the dishes. (*wash*)

3 What _____ she done?

_____ _____ a letter. (*write*)

4 What's _____ done?

_____ _____ the milk. (*drink*)

5 What's he done?

_____ _____ the windows. (*clean*)

6 What have they done?

_____ _____ the window! (*break*)

ANSWERS
1 They've seen a film. **2** What has he done? He's washed the dishes. **3** What has she done? She's written a letter. **4** What's it done? It's drunk the milk. **5** He's cleaned the windows. **6** They've broken the window.

63 Verbs: present perfect or past simple?

I have done/ I did

We use the *present perfect tense* to talk about our experience.
We use the *past simple tense* when we say *when*.

Examples:

Have you ever been to Paris?
(there/in 1987)
Yes, I have, *I went* there in 1987.

Have you ever eaten snails? (   )
No, *I haven't*.

Have you ever seen a penguin? (one/in
London Zoo)
Yes, I have. *I saw* one in London Zoo.

Make a question and answer as in the examples above.

1 climb a high mountain   (one/when I was at school)

_____ ?   Yes, _____

2 swim in the Mediterranean   (in it/last year)

_____ ?   Yes, _____

3 catch a fish   (one/last Sunday afternoon)

_____ ?   Yes, _____

4 work in a hospital   (in one/as a student)

_____ ?   Yes, _____

5 play baseball   (   )

_____ ?   No, _____

6 win a lot of money   (a lot/in 1977)

_____ ?   Yes, _____

7 drink whisky   (some/yesterday evening)

_____ ?   Yes, _____

8 ride a motorbike   (one/when I was on holiday)

_____ ?   Yes, _____

9 shoot an animal   (   )

_____ ?   No, _____

10 go skiing   (last Christmas)

_____ ?   Yes, _____

11 paint a picture   (one/at primary school)

_____ ?   Yes, _____

12 sleep in a tent   (in one/last summer)

_____ ?   Yes, _____

ANSWERS
1 Have you ever climbed a mountain? Yes, I have. I climbed one when I was at school. 2 Have you ever swum in the Mediterranean? Yes, I have. I swam in it last year. 3 Have you ever caught a fish? Yes, I have. I caught one last Sunday afternoon. 4 Have you ever worked in a hospital? Yes, I have. I worked in one as a student. 5 Have you ever played baseball? No, I haven't. 6 Have you ever won a lot of money? Yes, I have. I won a lot in 1977. 7 Have you ever drunk whisky? Yes, I have. I drank some yesterday evening. 8 Have you ever ridden a motorbike? Yes, I have. I rode one when I was on holiday. 9 Have you ever shot an animal? No, I haven't. 10 Have you ever been skiing? Yes, I have. I went skiing last Christmas. 11 Have you ever painted a picture? Yes, I have. I painted one at primary school. 12 Have you ever slept in a tent? Yes, I have. I slept in one last summer.

64

Verbs: present simple

I *sleep*/ he *sleeps*

STATEMENT		NEGATIVE			QUESTION			SHORT ANSWER		
I You We They	sleep.	I You We They	don't.	sleep.	Do	I you we they	sleep?	Yes,	I you we they	do.
								No,		don't.
He She It	sleeps.	He She It	doesn't		Does	he she it		Yes,	he she it	does.
								No,		doesn't.

The *present simple tense* is used to describe things we do regularly, every day.

What do the Smith family do every day?

Mr Smith goes to bed at 11 o'clock.

Mr Smith reads the newspaper.
The children go to bed at 9 o'clock.

The children finish school.
Mr Smith doesn't finish work.

The children go home for lunch.
Mr Smith stays at work.

At 7 o'clock Mr Smith gets up.

At 8 o'clock the children get up.
At 8.30 Mr Smith goes to work.
At 9 o'clock the children go to school.

At 10.30 am Mr Smith drinks coffee.
The children don't drink coffee; they play.

Use the diagram above to answer these questions.

1   What does Mr Smith do at 7 o'clock? _____
2   Do the children get up at 7 o'clock? _____
3   What does Mr Smith do at 8.30 am? _____
4   Do the children drink coffee at 10.30 am? _____
5   What do the children do at 10.30 am? _____
6   Do the children go home for lunch? _____
7   Does Mr Smith finish work at 3.30 pm? _____
8   What does Mr Smith do in the evening? _____
9   When do the children go to bed? _____
10 Does Mr Smith go to bed at 11 o'clock? _____

ANSWERS
1 He gets up. 2 No, they don't. 3 He goes to work. 4 No, they don't. 5 They play.
6 Yes, they do. 7 No, he doesn't. 8 He reads the newspaper. 9 They go to bed at 9 o'clock. 10 Yes, he does.

65 Verbs: to be

I am. . ., It is. . .

STATEMENT	
I	am . . . 'm . . . am not . . .
You We They	are. . . 're. . . aren't. . .
He She It	is. . . 's. . . isn't. . .

QUESTION		
Am Aren't	I	?
Are Aren't	you we they	?
Is Isn't	he she it	?

SHORT ANSWER		
Yes, No,	I	am. 'm not.
Yes, No,	you we they	are. aren't.
Yes, No,	he she it	is. isn't.

Exercise A

To be + ADJECTIVE *Example*: He is angry!

Complete the sentences choosing from the adjectives given below.

cold	rich	strong	beautiful	tired	happy

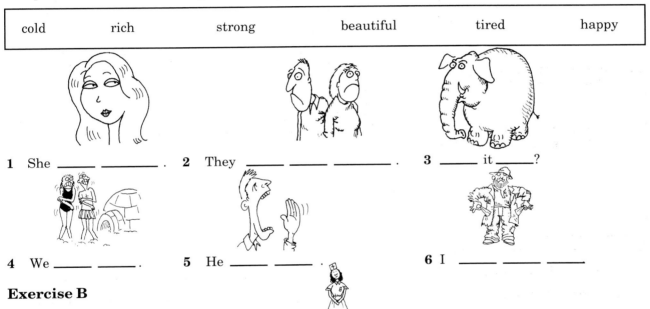

1 She _____ _____ .
2 They _____ _____ .
3 _____ it _____?

4 We _____ _____ .
5 He _____ _____ .
6 I _____ _____ _____

Exercise B

To be + NOUN *Example*: She is a nurse.

a student	a police officer	a champion	footballers	singers	a painter

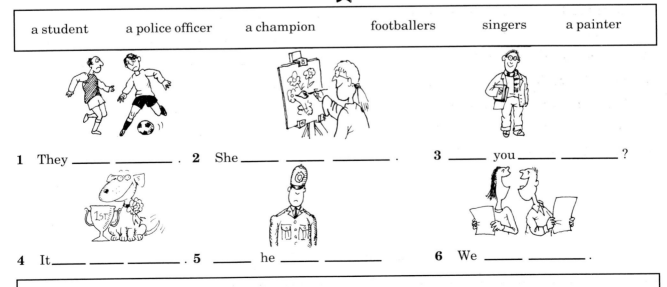

1 They _____ _____ .
2 She _____ _____ .
3 _____ you _____?

4 It _____ _____ .
5 _____ he _____ .
6 We _____ _____ .

He said he *would come.*

If the *speaking* verb is in the past tense, all the verbs which follow it must be in a past tense.

DIRECT SPEECH	REPORTED SPEECH	SPEAKING VERBS	
am / is / are do / does have done did will do	was did has done had done would do	he *said* he *told* him they *explained* we *asked* I *replied*	(We can use *that* after the speaking verb, but we often leave it out.)

Examples:

'I am going home', said Maria. (*say*)   *Maria said she was going home.*

'Ankara is in Turkey', my teacher said. (*tell*)   *My teacher told me that Ankara was in Turkey.*

'Is it raining?' she asked. (*ask*)   *She asked if it was raining.*

Exercise A

Read this dialogue and change it into reported speech. Use *he / she*, *him / her* after the first two sentences.

Example: *Maria*: I'm having a party this evening, José. (*tell*)
Maria told José that she was having a party that evening.

1 *José*: Where are you having it?   (*ask*)

_____

2 *Maria*: It's at the Youth Club. Can you come?   (*reply / ask*)

_____

3 *José*: Yes, I can, but I don't know where it is.   (*say*)

_____

4 *Maria*: It's next to the Catholic Church. It will start at 9 o'clock.   (*explain*)

_____

5 *José*: I have a piano lesson until 9.30 but I'll come later.   (*say*)

_____

6 *Maria*: Have you seen Juan?   (*ask*)

_____

7 *José*: Juan went to Seville at 9 o'clock but he will be back by 5.   (*tell*)

_____

8 *Maria*: I want Juan to come. Will you ask him for me?   (*explain / ask*)

_____

9 *José*: I will only if you promise to dance with me.   (*reply*)

_____

10 *Maria*: I think you are jealous, José.   (*tell*)

_____

Exercise B

Do Exercise 21 on the cassette.

ANSWERS
A 1 José asked where she was having it. 2 Maria replied that it was at the Youth Club. She asked if he could come. 3 He said he could, but he didn't know where it was. 4 She explained that it was next to the Catholic Church and that it would start at 9 o'clock. 5 He said he had a piano lesson until 9.30, but he would come later. 6 She asked if he had seen Juan. 7 He told her that Juan had gone to Seville at 9 o'clock but he would be back by 5. 8 She explained that she wanted Juan to come. She asked José if he would ask him for her. 9 He replied that he would only if she promised to dance with him. 10 She told José that she thought he was jealous.

67 Verbs: there is and there are

There are many things.

We use *There is* . . . with singular or uncountable nouns.

There *is* (*There's*) _____a tree_____ in the garden.

a tree

some grass

an elephant

a dog

We use *There are* with plural nouns:

There *are* _____two trees_____ in the garden.

two trees

some flowers

a few people

a lot of birds

Two astronauts have landed on a strange planet. They are reporting to Earth about what they can see.
Fill in the blanks with *There is* or *There are*.

Hello, Earth. This planet is very interesting. I can see lots of things –

1 _____ _____ a dog with two heads.

2 _____ _____ some strange trees.

3 And _____ _____ two moons in the sky.

4 _____ _____ snow on the mountains.

5 _____ _____ a lot of holes in the ground.

6 _____ _____ a few houses in the distance.

7 And _____ _____ some smoke coming from them.

8 _____ _____ some vehicles outside the houses.

9 And _____ _____ a lot of noise.

10 I think _____ _____ a party going on!

ANSWERS
1 There is; 2 There are; 3 there are; 4 There is; 5 There are; 6 There are; 7 there is; 8 There are; 9 there is;
10 there is.

Exercise A

Write the meaning in your own language.

Infinitive	Past	Past participle	Meaning in your language	Infinitive	Past	Past participle	Meaning in your language
be	was	been	_____	lose	lost	lost	_____
begin	began	begun	_____	make	made	made	_____
bite	bit	bitten	_____	mean	meant	meant	_____
break	broke	broken	_____	meet	met	met	_____
bring	brought	brought	_____	pay	paid	paid	_____
buy	bought	bought	_____	put	put	put	_____
catch	caught	caught	_____	read	read	read	_____
choose	chose	chosen	_____	ride	rode	ridden	_____
come	came	come	_____	run	ran	run	_____
cost	cost	cost	_____	say	said	said	_____
drink	drank	drunk	_____	see	saw	seen	_____
drive	drove	driven	_____	sell	sold	sold	_____
eat	ate	eaten	_____	send	sent	sent	_____
fall	fell	fallen	_____	show	showed	shown	_____
feel	felt	felt	_____	shoot	shot	shot	_____
find	found	found	_____	shut	shut	shut	_____
fly	flew	flown	_____	sing	sang	sung	_____
forget	forgot	forgotten	_____	sit	sat	sat	_____
get	got	got	_____	speak	spoke	spoken	_____
give	gave	given	_____	spend	spent	spent	_____
go	went	gone	_____	stand	stood	stood	_____
grow	grew	grown	_____	swim	swam	swum	_____
have	had	had	_____	take	took	taken	_____
hear	heard	heard	_____	teach	taught	taught	_____
hold	held	held	_____	tell	told	told	_____
keep	kept	kept	_____	think	thought	thought	_____
know	knew	known	_____	understand	understood	understood	_____
leave	left	left	_____	wear	wore	worn	_____
let	let	let	_____	write	wrote	written	_____

 ## Exercise B

Do Exercise 22 on the cassette.

Tapescript 1

Exercise 1 Adjectives: comparison

Look at Worksheet 2.

Listen to this example.

Who is fatter – Mr Adams or Mr Church?
Mr Adams is fatter than Mr Church.

Now you answer. First, listen to the example again and answer.

Who is fatter – Mr Adams or Mr Church?
Mr Adams is fatter than Mr Church.

1   Who is thinner – Miss Brookes or Ms Dangerfield?
Miss Brookes is thinner than Ms Dangerfield.

2   Who is happier – Mr Church or Mr Adams?
Mr Church is happier than Mr Adams.

3   Who is sadder – Ms Dangerfield or Miss Brookes?
Ms Dangerfield is sadder than Miss Brookes.

4   Who is richer – Mr Church or Mr Adams?
Mr Church is richer than Mr Adams.

5   Who is poorer – Ms Dangerfield or Miss Brookes?
Ms Dangerfield is poorer than Miss Brookes.

6   Who is more intelligent – Mr Adams or Miss Brookes?
Mr Adams is more intelligent than Miss Brookes.

7   Who is stronger – Mr Church or Ms Dangerfield?
Mr Church is stronger than Ms Dangerfield.

Tapescript 2

Exercise 2 Adjectives: possessive

Look at Worksheet 3.

First, listen to the dialogue from the worksheet.

Diane: Who is the man in the centre?
Mary: It's my husband, David.
Diane: Is Joan your sister?
Mary: No – she's my mother!
Diane: And is Anne your daughter?
Mary: No, she's my niece.
Diane: Is Peter her brother?
Mary: No, he's her cousin.
Diane: And who's Joe?
Mary: He's her brother.
Diane: Is Louise Fred's sister?
Mary: No, she's his wife.
Diane: So, is Louise your sister?
Mary: Yes, she is.
Diane: And Peter is your son?
Mary: Yes, he is.
Diane: So that means David is Peter and Sue's uncle?
Mary: No! He's my husband – their father.
Diane: And this person, Arthur, is your and Louise's brother?
Mary: No! He's our father!
Diane: Your mother looks very young – you have a very nice family.
Mary: Thank you.

Now listen carefully to these examples.

Diane: Who does this book belong to?
Mary: Me.
Diane: Oh, so it's your book.
Diane: Who do these shoes belong to?
Mary: You.
Diane: Oh, so they're my shoes.

Now you answer.

Diane: 1. Who does this book belong to?
Mary: Me.
Diane: Oh, so it's your book.
Diane: 2. Who do these shoes belong to?
Mary: You.
Diane: Oh, so they're my shoes.
Diane: 3. Who does this knife belong to?
Mary: David.
Diane: Oh, so it's his knife.
Diane: 4. Who do these gloves belong to?
Mary: Louise.
Diane: Oh, so they're her gloves.
Diane: 5. Who does this car belong to?
Mary: Louise and Fred.
Diane: Oh, so it's their car.
Diane: 6. Who do these coats belong to?
Mary: You and me.
Diane: Oh, so they're our coats.

Tapescript 3

Exercise 3 Adjectives: superlative

Look at Worksheet 4.

Listen to this example.

A: Which is the highest mountain in the world – Mount Everest?
B: Yes, Mount Everest is definitely the highest mountain in the world.

Now you give the answers.

1   Which is the longest river in Europe – the Danube?
    Yes, the Danube is definitely the longest river in Europe.

2   Which is the biggest animal in Africa – the elephant?
    Yes, the elephant is definitely the biggest animal in Africa.

3   Which is the busiest airport in England – Heathrow?
    Yes, Heathrow is definitely the busiest airport in England.

4   Which is the most expensive metal in the world – platinum?
    Yes, platinum is definitely the most expensive metal in the world.

5   Which is the fastest passenger plane in the world – Concorde?
    Yes, Concorde is definitely the fastest passenger plane in the world.

Tapescript 4

Exercise 4 Adverbs: formation

Look at Worksheet 6.

Listen to this example.

A: Isn't Susan a careful driver!
B: Yes, she always drives carefully.

Now you respond in the same way.

  1 Isn't John a quick runner!
     Yes, he always runs quickly.

  2 Isn't Mohammed a brave fighter!
     Yes, he always fights bravely.

  3 Isn't Geoffrey a bad writer!
     Yes, he always writes badly.

  4 Isn't Maria a beautiful singer!
     Yes, she always sings beautifully.

  5 Isn't Sheila a strong swimmer!
     Yes, she always swims strongly.

  6 Isn't Andy a noisy eater!
     Yes, he always eats noisily.

  7 Isn't Ilanova a graceful dancer!
     Yes, she always dances gracefully.

  8 Isn't Anne a dangerous driver!
     Yes, she always drives dangerously.

  9 Isn't Joe a careless painter!
     Yes, he always paints carelessly.

 10 Isn't the bird a loud singer!
     Yes, it always sings loudly.

Tapescript 5

Exercise 5 Nouns: countable/uncountable

Look at Worksheet 12.

Jim is going shopping. Mary wants him to buy some things for her.

Mary:	Let's see – I need some milk – Two pints.
Jim:	Two pints of milk. Anything else?
Mary:	Yes. I need some biscuits.
Jim:	OK. Some milk and some biscuits. Anything else?
Mary:	Oh yes. I need a cabbage.
Jim:	OK. Some milk, some biscuits and a cabbage. Anything else?

Now you take the part of Jim.

Mary:	Let's see – I need some milk – Two pints.
Jim:	Two pints of milk. Anything else?
Mary:	Yes. I need some biscuits.
Jim:	OK. Some milk and some biscuits. Anything else?
Mary:	Oh yes. I need a cabbage.
Jim:	OK. Some milk, some biscuits and a cabbage. Anything else?
Mary:	Oh yes. I need some cheese.
Jim:	OK. Some milk, some biscuits, a cabbage and some cheese. Anything else?
Mary:	Oh yes – I need a chicken.
Jim:	OK. Some milk, some biscuits, a cabbage, some cheese and a chicken. Anything else?
Mary:	Oh yes – I need some wine.
Jim:	OK. Some milk, some biscuits, a cabbage, some cheese, a chicken and some wine. Anything else?
Mary:	Oh yes, a newspaper.
Jim:	OK. Some milk, some biscuits, a cabbage, some cheese, a chicken, some wine and a newspaper. Anything else?
Mary:	No, thank you, dear. That's all.

Tapescript 6

Exercise 6 Prepositions: direction

Look at Worksheet 13.

Jim knows that Pierre is very strong and fit. He wants to know what he does to get fit.

Jim: What does Pierre do every morning?
John: At 6.30 he goes to the start line.
Jim: And what does he do next?
John: He runs along a track towards a river.

Now you answer the questions.

Jim: What does Pierre do every morning?
John: At 6.30 he goes to the start line.
Jim: And what does he do next?
John: He runs along a track towards a river.
Jim: And then what does he do?
John: He climbs up a tree.
Jim: And after that?
John: He goes across the river on a rope bridge.
Jim: And what does he do next?
John: He climbs over a wall and into a tunnel.
Jim: And then?
John: He goes through the tunnel.
Jim: And what does he do when he comes out of it?
John: He crawls under barbed wire.
Jim: And what does he do after that?
John: He runs down a hill and jumps onto a platform.
Jim: And then?
John: He jumps off the platform into the water.
Jim: And after that?
John: He runs through the water and back to the start line.
Jim: He must be crazy!!

Tapescript 7

Exercise 7 Prepositions: time

Look at Worksheet 16.

Listen to this dialogue.

A: It's seven o'clock. Do you go to work about now?
B: No, I never go to work at seven o'clock.
A: It's Sunday. Don't you play golf today?
B: No, I never play golf on Sunday.

Now you answer.

1 It's seven o'clock. Do you go to work about now?
  No, I never go to work at seven o'clock.

2 It's Sunday. Don't you play golf today?
  No, I never play golf on Sunday.

3 It's one o'clock. Don't you have lunch about now?
  No, I never have lunch at one o'clock.

4 It's winter. Don't you wear a hat?
  No, I never wear a hat in winter.

5 It's Christmas. Don't you normally go to Spain?
  No, I never go to Spain at Christmas.

6 It's Thursday. Don't you usually go home early?
  No, I never go home early on Thursday.

7 It's the fourth of July. Don't you normally have a party today?
  No, I never have a party on the fourth of July.

8 It's nearly half past eight. Don't you go to the pub about now?
  No, I never go to the pub at half past eight.

9 It's Saturday evening. Don't you generally go out?
  No, I never go out on Saturday evening.

10 It's a quarter past five. Don't you usually leave the office about now?
  No, I never leave the office at quarter past five.

Tapescript 8

Exercise 8 Pronouns: compound

Look at Worksheet 17.

Mary has just arrived back from her holiday. John has been looking after her flat for her. Listen.

Mary: Did anybody phone while I was away?
John: No, nobody phoned.
Mary: Did anything exciting happen while I was away?
John: No, nothing exciting happened.

Now you take the part of John.

Mary: Did anybody phone while I was away?
John: No, nobody phoned.
Mary: Did anything exciting happen while I was away?
John: No, nothing exciting happened.
Mary: Did anybody leave any messages?
John: No, nobody left any messages.
Mary: Did anything arrive for me?
John: No, nothing arrived for you.
Mary: Did anybody ask about me?
John: No, nobody asked about you.
Mary: Did anybody say anything about me?
John: No, nobody said anything about you.
Mary: Did anything go wrong?
John: No, nothing went wrong.
Mary: Well, I wish something had happened!

Tapescript 9

Exercise 9 Pronouns: possessive

Look at Worksheet 19.

Mr Brown has a bad memory. He's at the airport with his family trying to sort out all the suitcases. Listen.

Mr Brown: Let's sort out these suitcases. I can't remember whose is whose. What colour did you have, John?
John: Blue.
Mr Brown: Oh yes, so this is yours.
John: And Mary had a green one.
Mr Brown: Oh yes, so this is hers.

Now you answer for Mr Brown.

Mr Brown: Let's sort out these suitcases. I can't remember whose is whose. What colour did you have, John?
John: Blue.
Mr Brown: Oh yes, so this is yours.
John: And Mary had a green one.
Mr Brown: Oh yes, so this is hers.
John: And the children had a black one.
Mr Brown: Oh yes, so this is theirs.
John: And Mum had a light blue one.
Mr Brown: Oh yes, so this is hers.
John: And Uncle Charles had a dark brown one.
Mr Brown: Oh yes, so this is his.
John: And you had a light brown one.
Mr Brown: Oh yes, so this is mine.
John: And we also brought an extra striped one.
Mr Brown: Oh yes, so this is ours. Now, where is the taxi?

Andy and Audrey Jackson: Elementary Grammar Worksheets Photocopy Masters © Prentice Hall International (UK) Ltd 1992. All rights reserved

Tapescript 10

Exercise 10 Pronouns: reflexive

Look at Worksheet 20.

John is always trying to help everybody. But his father doesn't want him to. Listen to the dialogue.

John: Shall I help you wash the car, Dad?
Dad: No, thanks, son. I can do it myself.
John: Well, shall I give Mum a hand with the dinner?
Dad: No, thanks, son. She can do it herself.

Now you are John's Dad.

John: Shall I help you wash the car, Dad?
Dad: No, thanks, son. I can do it myself.
John: Well, shall I give Mum a hand with the dinner?
Dad: No, thanks, son. She can do it herself.
John: Well, shall I help the girls do their homework?
Dad: No, thanks, son. They can do it themselves.
John: Well, shall I help Grandad lay the table?
Dad: No, thanks, son. He can do it himself.
John: Well, shall I help the dog find its bone?
Dad: No, thanks, son. It can do it itself.
John: Well, shall I help Mum tidy the room?
Dad: No, thanks, son. She can do it herself.
John: Well, can I give you a hand with the painting?
Dad: No, thanks, son. I can do it myself.
John: Well, can you help me clean my room?
Dad: No, thanks, son. You can do it yourself!

Andy and Audrey Jackson: Elementary Grammar Worksheets Photocopy Masters © Prentice Hall International (UK) Ltd 1992. All rights reserved

Tapescript 11

Exercise 11   Quantifiers: a little/a few

Look at Worksheet 21.

Jane and Mary are students. They don't have much money, but Jane likes shopping. She wants to buy food, but Mary thinks they have enough. Listen.

Jane: Shall I get some more biscuits?
Mary: No, we've still got a few. We can get some more next week.
Jane: How about some more butter?
Mary: No, we've still got a little. We can get some more next week.

Now you answer for Mary.

Jane: Shall I get some more biscuits?
Mary: No, we've still got a few. We can get some more next week.
Jane: How about some more butter?
Mary: No, we've still got a little. We can get some more next week.
Jane: Well, shall I buy some bananas?
Mary: No, we've still got a few. We can buy some more next week.
Jane: OK. So I'll get some more cheese.
Mary: No, we've still got a little. We can get some more next week.
Jane: All right. So shall I get some more milk?
Mary: No, we've still got a little. We can get some more next week.
Jane: If you say so. But how about some more eggs?
Mary: No, we've still got a few. We can get some more next week.
Jane: OK. What if I get some more potatoes?
Mary: No, we've still got a few left. We can get some more next week.
Jane: So what if I go to the bank and get some more money?
Mary: No, we've still got a little left. We can get some more next week.
Jane: OK. So let's just stay at home and watch the TV!!

Andy and Audrey Jackson: Elementary Grammar Worksheets Photocopy Masters © Prentice Hall International (UK) Ltd 1992. All rights reserved

Tapescript 12

Exercise 12 Quantifiers: a lot of/much/many

Look at Worksheet 23.

Jane is talking about her boyfriends with Mary.

Jane: I like John. He's got a lot of cars.
Mary: Yes, but he hasn't got much patience.

Now you take the part of Mary.

Jane: I like John. He's got a lot of cars.
Mary: Yes, but he hasn't got much patience.
Jane: I like David. He's got a lot of money.
Mary: Yes, but he hasn't got many friends.
Jane: I like Michael. He's got a lot of charm.
Mary: Yes, but he hasn't got much money.
Jane: I like Arthur. He's a lot of fun.
Mary: Yes, but he hasn't got much sense of fashion.
Jane: I like Bill. He's a lot of fun.
Mary: Yes, but he hasn't got many clothes.
Jane: I like Syd. He's got a lot of style.
Mary: Yes, but he hasn't got much humour.
Jane: I like Fred. He's got a lot of luck.
Mary: Yes, but he hasn't got much style.
Jane: Oh, you're impossible, Mary. You don't like any of my friends!

Tapescript 13

Exercise 13 Questions: indirect

Look at Worksheet 27.

Maria is in London for the first time. She needs a lot of information, so she asks a police officer. Listen.

Maria:	I wonder what time it is. I'll ask that police officer. Excuse me . . .
Police officer:	Yes?
Maria:	Could you tell me what time it is?
Police officer:	Certainly. It's two o'clock.

Now you take over the part of Maria.

1 Maria: I wonder what time it is. I'll ask that police officer. Excuse me . . .
  Police officer: Yes?
  Maria: Could you tell me what time it is?
  Police officer: Certainly. It's two o'clock.
  Maria: Thank you.

2 Maria: I wonder where the post office is. I'll ask that police officer. Excuse me . . .
  Police officer: Yes?
  Maria: Could you tell me where the post office is?
  Police officer: Certainly. It's just round the corner on the left.
  Maria: Thank you.

3 Maria: I wonder if the pubs are open. I'll ask that police officer. Excuse me . . .
  Police officer: Yes?
  Maria: Could you tell me if the pubs are open?
  Police officer: Certainly. They are open until 3 o'clock.
  Maria: Thank you.

4 Maria: I wonder if there's a toilet near here. I'll ask that police officer. Excuse me . . .
  Police officer: Yes?
  Maria: Could you tell me if there is a toilet near here?
  Police officer: Certainly. There's one just over there.
  Maria: Thank you.

5 Maria: I wonder how far the station is. I'll ask that police officer. Excuse me . . .
  Police officer: Yes?
  Maria: Could you tell me how far the station is?
  Police officer: Certainly. It's about half a mile from here.
  Maria: Thank you.

6 Maria: I wonder when the bank opens. I'll ask that police officer. Excuse me . . .
  Police officer: Yes?
  Maria: Could you tell me when the bank opens?
  Police officer: Certainly. At half past nine.
  Maria: Thank you.

7 Maria: I wonder if I can cross the road here. I'll ask that police officer. Excuse me . . .
  Police officer: Yes?
  Maria: Could you tell me if I can cross the road here?
  Police officer: Certainly. But wait until the lights change.
  Maria: Thank you.

8 Maria: I wonder when the shops close. I'll ask that police officer. Excuse me . . .
  Police officer: Yes?
  Maria: Could you tell me when the shops close?
  Police officer: Certainly. Most of them close at six.
  Maria: Thank you.

Tapescript 14

Exercise 14 Responses: so do I, neither do I

Look at Worksheet 33.

Manuel and Giovanni are two students who seem to be like each other. Listen.

Manuel:　I can't swim.
Giovanni: Neither can I.
Manuel:　I have two cars.
Giovanni: So have I.

Now you take the part of Giovanni.

Manuel:　I can't swim.
Giovanni: Neither can I.
Manuel:　I have two cars.
Giovanni: So have I.
Manuel:　My father has a big company.
Giovanni: So has mine.
Manuel:　I have two sisters.
Giovanni: So have I.
Manuel:　I'll be here until Christmas.
Giovanni: So will I.
Manuel:　I don't like English food.
Giovanni: Neither do I.
Manuel:　My host family is very friendly.
Giovanni: So is mine.
Manuel:　I've done all my homework.
Giovanni: So have I.
Manuel:　I went to the disco last night.
Giovanni: So did I.
Manuel:　My teacher doesn't eat meat.
Giovanni: Neither does mine.

Tapescript 15

Exercise 15 Verbs: future with `going to'

Look at Worksheet 36.

It's Friday afternoon. Mary and David are discussing what is going to happen this evening. Listen.

Mary: She always reads a book on Friday evenings.
David: So that means she's going to read a book this evening.
Mary: He never plays the drums on Friday evenings.
David: So that means he's not going to play the drums this evening.

Now you take David's part.

Mary: She always reads a book on Friday evenings.
David: So that means she's going to read a book this evening.
Mary: He never plays the drums on Friday evenings.
David: So that means he's not going to play the drums this evening.
Mary: They always watch TV on Friday evenings.
David: So that means they're going to watch TV this evening.
Mary: I never do my homework on Friday evenings.
David: So that means you're not going to do your homework this evening.
Mary: It always rains on Friday evenings.
David: So that means it's going to rain this evening.

Tapescript 16

Exercise 16 Verbs: Modal auxiliaries with 'have to'/'have got to'

Look at Worksheet 46.

Sally is a teacher and John is a shop assistant. They are being interviewed about what is necessary for their jobs. Listen.

Interviewer: What about university, Sally?
Sally: Yes, I've got to go to university.
Interviewer: And you, John?
John: No, I don't have to.

Now you answer the interviewer.

Interviewer: What about university, Sally?
Sally: Yes, I've got to go to university.
Interviewer: And you John?
John: No, I don't have to.
Interviewer: And what about working on Saturdays, Sally?
Sally: No, I don't have to work on Saturdays.
Interviewer: And you, John?
John: Yes, I've got to.
Interviewer: And what about marking homework?
Sally: Yes, I've got to mark homework.
Interviewer: And you, John?
John: No, I don't have to.
Interviewer: And what about writing reports, Sally?
Sally: Yes, I've got to write reports.
Interviewer: And you, John?
John: No, I don't have to.
Interviewer: And what about serving customers, Sally?
Sally: No, I don't have to serve customers.
Interviewer: And you, John?
John: Yes, I've got to.
Interviewer: And what about taking money, Sally?
Sally: No, I don't have to take money.
Interviewer: And you, John?
John: Yes, I've got to.

Tapescript 17

Exercise 17 Verbs: passive, past simple

Look at Worksheet 50.

Agree with the speaker, but change the sentence. Listen to this example.

A: Bombs killed many people during the war.
B: Many people were killed during the war.

Now you respond.

A: Bombs killed many people during the war.
B: Many people were killed during the war.
A: Someone made this car in Japan.
B: This car was made in Japan.
A: The gardener didn't cut the grass this morning.
B: The grass wasn't cut this morning.
A: The teacher didn't correct the exam papers last night.
B: The exam papers weren't corrected last night.
A: Did someone invite the Queen to the wedding?
B: Was the Queen invited to the wedding?

Tapescript 18

Exercise 18 Verbs: past habitual

Look at Worksheet 53.

David and Mike have just met in a pub. Listen.

David: I live in a small flat.
Mike: Really? I used to live in a small flat, but not now.
David: I work in an office.
Mike: Really? I used to work in an office, but not now.

Now you take the part of Mike.

David: I live in a small flat.
Mike: Really? I used to live in a small flat, but not now.
David: I work in an office.
Mike: Really? I used to work in an office, but not now.
David: I play football every Saturday.
Mike: Really? I used to play football, but not now.
David: I have a lot of friends.
Mike: Really? I used to have a lot of friends, but not now.
David: I drink beer.
Mike: Really? I used to drink beer, but not now.
David: I wear jeans.
Mike: Really? I used to wear jeans, but not now.
David: I read the Sun newspaper.
Mike: Really? I used to read the Sun newspaper, but not now.
David: I enjoy life.
Mike: Really? I used to enjoy life, but not now.

Tapescript 19

Exercise 19 Verbs: past simple with regular verbs

Look at Worksheet 55.

The Smith family do the same things every day. What did they do yesterday? Listen.

A: What did the children do at 8.15?
B: They washed their hands and faces.

Now you answer.

A: What did the children do at 8.15?
B: They washed their hands and faces.
A: What did Mr Smith do at 9 o'clock?
B: He arrived at the office.
A: What did the children do at 10 o'clock?
B: They played with their friends.
A: What did Mr Smith do at 12.30?
B: He walked to the pub for lunch.
A: What did the children do at 3.30?
B: They finished school.
A: What did Mr Smith do at 7 o'clock?
B: He cleaned the car.
A: What did the children do at 8.30?
B: They cleaned their teeth.
A: And what did Mr Smith do at 10 o'clock?
B: He talked to his wife.

Tapescript 20

Exercise 20 Verbs: present perfect continuous

Look at Worksheet 61.

The Smith family are very tired. They have been working all day. Listen.

A: Why is Mr Smith tired?
B: He's been driving all day.

Now you answer the questions.

A: Why is Mr Smith tired?
B: He's been driving all day.
A: Why is Mrs Smith so tired?
B: She's been gardening all day.
A: Why are the children so tired?
B: They've been playing football all day.
A: Why is the dog so tired?
B: It's been chasing the cat all day.
A: Why are Grandma and Grandpa so tired?
B: They've been walking in the park all day.

Andy and Audrey Jackson: Elementary Grammar Worksheets Photocopy Masters © Prentice Hall International (UK) Ltd 1992. All rights reserved

Tapescript 21

Exercise 21 Reported speech

Look at Worksheet 66.

Maria was speaking on the phone to José What did they say? Listen.

Maria:	I'm having a party this evening, José.
Presenter:	What did she tell him?
A:	She told him that she was having a party.

Now you answer.

Maria:	I'm having a party this evening, José.
Presenter:	What did she tell him?
A:	She told him that she was having a party.
José:	Where are you having it?
Presenter:	What did he ask her?
A:	He asked her where she was having it.
Maria:	It's at the Youth Club.
Presenter:	What did she reply?
A:	She replied that it was at the Youth Club.
Maria:	Can you come?
Presenter:	What did she ask him?
A:	She asked him if he could come.
José:	Yes, I can, but I don't know where it is.
Presenter:	What did he say?
A:	He said that he could, but he didn't know where it was.
Maria:	It's next to the Catholic Church.
Presenter:	What did she explain?
A:	She explained that it was next to the Catholic Church.
Maria:	It will start at 9 o'clock.
Presenter:	What did she tell him?
A:	She told him that it would start at 9 o'clock.
José:	I have a piano lesson until 9.30, but I'll come later.
Presenter:	What did he say?
A:	He said he had a piano lesson until 9.30, but he would come later.

Tapescript 22

Exercise 22 Irregular verb table

Look at Worksheet 68.

This exercise is to help you to pronounce the parts of the irregular verbs. Repeat the parts after the speaker.

be	was	been	begin	began	begun	bite	bit	bitten
break	broke	broken	bring	brought	brought	buy	bought	brought
catch	caught	caught	choose	chose	chosen	come	came	come
cost	cost	cost	drink	drank	drunk	drive	drove	driven
eat	ate	eaten	fall	fell	fallen	feel	felt	felt
find	found	found	fly	flew	flown	forget	forgot	forgotten
get	got	got	give	gave	given	go	went	gone
grow	grew	grown	have	had	had	hear	heard	heard
hold	held	held	keep	kept	kept	know	knew	known
leave	left	left	let	let	let	lose	lost	lost
make	made	made	mean	meant	meant	meet	met	met
pay	paid	paid	put	put	put	read	read	read
ride	rode	ridden	run	ran	run	say	said	said
see	saw	seen	sell	sold	sold	send	sent	sent
show	showed	shown	shoot	shot	shot	shut	shut	shut
sing	sang	sung	sit	sat	sat	speak	spoke	spoken
spend	spent	spent	stand	stood	stood	swim	swam	swum
take	took	taken	teach	taught	taught	tell	told	told
think	thought	thought	understand	understood	understood	wear	wore	worn
write	wrote	written						

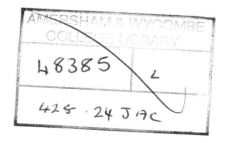
Andy and Audrey Jackson: Elementary Grammar Worksheets Photocopy Masters © Prentice Hall International (UK) Ltd 1992. All rights reserved